MINDFULNESS FOR STRESS MANAGEMENT

A Direct Path Through Brain Training to Overcome Panic Attacks,
Anxiety, and Overcoming Stress.
Anxiety Relief, Give Up Negative Thinking.

BARBRA BALDWIN

Table of Content

Chapter 1

All of us enjoy stress in our lives. Because the enormous majority of health issues is brought on or inspired using stress, it's vital to understand how pressure influences your frame and learn effective stress control strategies to make pressure just right for you in place of in opposition to you.

What is stress?

Stress is your frame's reaction to adjustments to your life. Because life entails regular trade (starting from changing locations from domestic to work each morning to adapting to predominant lifestyles modifications like marriage, divorce, or demise of a cherished one), there may be no warding off pressure.1 that is why your intention should not be to get rid of all stress however to dispose of useless pressure and efficiently control the relaxation. There are a few common reasons for stress that many humans experience, but all of us are extraordinary.

Causes of stress

Stress can come from many resources, which can be referred to as "stressors." because our experience of what is considered "stressful" is created through our particular perceptions of what we come upon in life (primarily based on our mix of character tendencies, to be had resources, ordinary concept styles), a state of affairs may be perceived as "disturbing" via one person and simply "hard" by way of a person else.

Without a doubt put, one man or woman's stress cause may not register as annoying to someone else. That said, certain conditions tend to cause greater stress in the majority and may grow the chance of burnout. As an example, when we find ourselves in situations wherein there are excessive demands on us; where we've little control, and few alternatives; wherein we do not feel prepared; in which we can be harshly judged through others; and wherein results for failure are steep or unpredictable, we generally tend to get stressed.

Due to this, many people are burdened by way of their jobs, their relationships, their economic troubles, health issues, and greater mundane things like litter or busy schedules. Getting to know abilities to deal with these stressors can assist lessen your revel in of stress?

Effects of pressure

Just as pressure is perceived differently by using each people, stress affects us all in approaches that are particular to us.

One individual may enjoy complications; at the same time as another can also locate stomach disenchanted is a common response, and a third might also enjoy any of some of the other symptoms. While all of us react to pressure in our very own methods, there is a long listing of generally experienced effects of stress that variety from moderate to lifestyles-threatening. Pressure can affect immunity that may certainly impact all areas of fitness. Pressure can affect temper in lots of ways as nicely.

In case you find yourself experiencing bodily signs, you think it can be associated with stress, talk for your physician to make sure you are doing what you could to shield your fitness. Signs and symptoms that can be exacerbated via pressure aren't "all in your head" and want to be taken critically.

Creating a pressure management plan is often one a part of a plan for average wellness.

Powerful stress control

Stress can be efficaciously managed in lots of one-of-a-kind approaches. The best stress control plans commonly include a mixture of stress relievers that cope with stress, bodily, and psychologically and assist in broadening resilience and coping capabilities.

7 Highly Effective Stress Relievers

Use quick stress relievers. Some pressure remedy techniques can work in only a few minutes to calm the frame's stress response. These techniques offer a "brief restoration" that helps you experience calmer in the meanwhile, and this could assist in several approaches. While your stress reaction is not brought on, you can technique problems more thoughtfully and proactively. You'll be much less likely to lash out at others out of frustration that may hold your relationships healthier. Nipping your pressure reaction inside the bud also can hold you from experiencing persistent stress.

Short pressure relievers like respiration exercises, for example, won't build your resilience to destiny stress or minimize the stressors that you face, but they could assist calm the frame's physiology as soon as the stress reaction is brought on.2

Expand pressure-relieving behavior. Some strategies are less handy to use while you are inside the center of a demanding state of affairs. However, if you exercise them often, they will let you manipulate stress in general by using being less reactive to it and extra capable of opposite your stress reaction quickly and effortlessly.

Lengthy-time period wholesome habits, like workout or ordinary meditation, can assist in promoting resilience in the direction of stressors in case you lead them to a regular a part of your life.3 communication capabilities and other lifestyle capabilities may be useful in handling stressors and converting how we feel from "overwhelmed" to "challenged" or even "stimulated."

Do away with stressors while you can. You could not be capable of absolutely remove pressure from your life or even the largest stressors; however, there are regions in which you can reduce it and get it to a manageable degree. Any stress that you may reduce out can minimize your overall stress load. For instance, ending even one toxic relationship lets you extra efficiently cope with other stress you enjoy because you can feel less beaten.

Coming across a huge sort of pressure management techniques, and then choosing a mixture that fits your desires, maybe a key method for powerful stress relief.

What is stress control?

Our more and busier lives motive our minds several stress. Stress is intellectual anxiety caused by disturbing, taxing, or burdensome circumstances. Stress does not just affect our mental country and temper; it influences our physical health as well. While we are much burdened, a hormone called cortisol is released into our bloodstream, suppressing the functioning of our immune, digestive, and reproductive structures. That is why it is so essential to exercise stress management to hold our minds and bodies healthful.

Pressure management consists of making adjustments to your existence if you are in a regular worrying state of affairs, stopping stress with the aid of practicing self-care and relaxation, and managing your reaction to disturbing situations after they do arise.

Before we move on to stress control strategies, it is crucial to be aware that not all stress is bad. Stress is a survival reaction, while our frame thinks that it's far in threat. This is why our sympathetic frightened gadget kicks in and makes our heart charge boom and gives us a burst of the strength hormone, adrenaline, so that we can deal with whatever situation is being thrown at us. That is also known as our flight or fight response.

The problem is when we address steady stress and fear, or while we do not know how to manipulate a worrying situation correctly. This is why stress management is enormously crucial for our fitness, first-class of lifestyles, and relationships.

Every word that a great laugh has a manner of lightening your burdens? Or perhaps you've skilled a situation like the sort of. Your day feels disturbing and overwhelming, but then you train yourself to step away from the rush, acquire your mind, make a listing of what's happening– prioritizing what's vital. Has your list ever helped you discover that perhaps your day is extra workable than it seemed? Or perhaps you commonly pass walking with a pal earlier than you begin your paintings day. This week seems too busy and traumatic to suit in such "frivolities." However, you decide that instead of skipping it, you'll cross ahead and walk. Afterward, you notice it turned into suitable for you bodily, socially, and emotionally and upon sitting down for the workday, you virtually experience extra able to attack the listing of obligations.

Discover ways to "pump the brakes" on pressure.

Laughter, physical interest, and organizing your thoughts may be powerful stress -control techniques. But something as easy as a quick smash also can be powerful. Dr. Robert Sapolsky, stress professional and neurology professor at Stanford, says all of us need to commit to everyday stress management and learn how to "pump the brakes" on pressure without loading it onto different people.

What is the purpose of stress?
Feelings are signals to help us apprehend troubles. Stress hormones help us combat-or-flee while we're in chance. But our frame's pressure reaction can end up a problem. At the same time, it continuously alerts danger approximately troubles that aren't always a risk, or it grows to the point of overwhelming our fitness, well-being, or clean thinking.

Why exercise pressure control?
Your thoughts deserve better than to be loaded down with the never-ending job of worrying! Some stress may be beneficial and can result in actual hassle-fixing; however, plenty of our stress is not sensible and even dangerous. Studies are

apparent that stressed brains do no longer operate in the same way as non-stressed brains. John Medina, Ph.D., director of the mind center for carried out gaining knowledge of studies at Seattle Pacific University, says creativity, productiveness, motivation, and occasionally even your immune system will all go through chronic stress.

How can we learn to manipulate our stress?

Step 1: attention! Study your "Low region. "Stress has a manner of turning into continual as the issues of normal living weigh us down. Or possibly you've grow to be accustomed to pressure for your lifestyles, and you allow whatever is presently the maximum stressful problem to dictate what you'll do every day. Absolutely everyone needs satisfaction, productiveness, and creativity in their lives, and chronic stress robs us of those.

In which do you place yourself now? How do you recognize while you've surpassed the mild factor? Pick out for yourself the small adjustments you could discover to your mood as you move up the continuum. This will take a few days of looking at yourself, but if you are like the general public (and possibilities are desirable that you are!), your stress degree will climb in a predictable pattern. In case you take time to research your emotional cues, you may learn to regulate your stress, so you spend more of sometime in the "low area".

However, you don't recognize how demanding my existence is!

Surely some humans have extra disturbing environments than others, and people will probably pay a toll on it until they discover ways to control stress and improve their first-class lifestyles. As an instance, the stress of turning into a caregiver often affects health difficulties and emotional fitness challenges. In case you are a caregiver, it's in particular critical which you study pressure-control competencies so that you can keep yourself inside the "low area," find ways to revel in your existence, and allow your caregiving to have moments of pride and joy.

Step 2: discover ways to stay inside the Low sector. Once you've handed the mid-area mark into the high-stress sector, it's time to take a pressure-management moment. Maybe that means which you call a pal, take a short 5-minute walk exterior, remind yourself of what you may and cannot exchange, or preserve a funny ebook on hand that you could visit while you need fun. Something works best for you; make an effort to deliver your stress level returned in the direction of the "low region." Be aware of what takes place for your body and thoughts while you are taking these breaks.

Is stress necessarily harmful to fitness?

Several specific sorts of stress range from eustress, which is a high-quality and thrilling shape of stress, to persistent stress, which has been connected to many extreme fitness issues and is the kind of terrible stress most customarily referred to in the news.1. At the same time, we want to manage or remove the bad types of stress; we also want to keep nice kinds of stress in our lives to help us stay essential and alive. However, if we revel in too much stress in our lives, even "true" stress can make contributions to immoderate stress levels that can cause feeling overwhelmed or having your stress reaction precipitated for too lengthy. That is why it is nonetheless important to discover ways to relax your frame and mind periodically and cut down on useless stress on every occasion viable.

How am I able to inform me when I'm too pressured?

Stress influences us all in specific approaches, now not all of which can be poor. (In fact, the stress of exciting lifestyles can function a very good motivator and keep things exciting.) While stress degrees get too excessive, however, there are some stress signs and symptoms that many humans revel in. For example, headaches, irritability, and 'fuzzy thinking' can all be signs and symptoms which you're underneath an excessive amount of pressure.1. At the same time, now not all and sundry who's underneath stress will enjoy those unique symptoms, many will. If you find which you don't realize how burdened you are till you are crushed, it's critical to learn to note your frame's subtle cues and your behavior, nearly like an outside observer would possibly. To note how your body is reacting to pressure, you could try this frame scan meditation (it helps relax at the identical time).

What am I able to Do once I feel beaten with the aid of pressure?

We all sense beaten once in a while; that's ordinary. While it's honestly not possible to remove instances when events conspire, and the body's pressure response is precipitated, there are methods that you could quick opposite your body's response to stress, buffering the harm on your health and retaining your thinking clean, so you can extra efficaciously deal with what's going on within the moment.

Is there a manner to Be much less suffering from pressure?

Surely, using practicing an everyday pressure control method or two, you could take away some of the stress you experience right now and make yourself greater resilient inside the face of stress in the future. There are several various things you can attempt, ranging from a morning stroll to an evening journaling exercise to just making more time for friends. The trick is to locate something that fits together with your lifestyle and personality, so it's less difficult to stick with.

Stress Management

At the same time, as it could seem like there's not anything you can do approximately stress at work and domestic, there are steps you can take to relieve the stress and regain manipulate.

Why is it so essential to manage pressure?

In case you're residing with excessive ranges of stress, you're placing your entire nicely-being at chance. Stress wreaks havoc to your emotional equilibrium, as well as your bodily health. It narrows your capability to assume actually, function efficaciously, and enjoy existence. It can seem like there's nothing you could do approximately stress. The bills won't stop coming, there will in no way be greater hours inside the day, and your paintings and circle of relative's responsibilities will continually be worrying. But you have a lot more manageable than you would possibly suppose.

Effective pressure management helps you destroy the maintained pressure has for your existence so that you can be happier, healthier, and extra productive. The remaining goal is a balanced life, with time for paintings, relationships, relaxation, and a laugh—and the resilience to maintain up under stress and meet demanding situations head-on. However, pressure management isn't one-size-fits-all. That's why it's important to experiment and find out what works excellent for you. The subsequent stress control guidelines will let you try this.

Tip 1: identify the sources of stress for your lifestyles

Pressure management begins with identifying the assets of stress for your lifestyles. This isn't as truthful as it sounds. At the same time, as it's smooth to identify important stressors consisting of changing jobs, transferring, or going through a divorce, pinpointing the assets of continual pressure can be extra complex. It's all too smooth to miss how your thoughts, emotions, and behaviors make contributions in your regular stress degrees. Positive, you can understand which you're continuously worried approximately work cut-off dates, however perhaps it's your procrastination, as opposed to the real job demands, that is inflicting the stress.

To pick out your real resources of pressure, appearance intently at your habits, mindset, and excuses:

Do you blame your stress on other human beings or outdoor activities, or view it as entirely normal and unexceptional?

Till you receive an obligation for the function you play in developing or preserving it, your stress degree will continue to be outdoor your manipulate.

Tip 2: exercise the four A's of pressure management

While stress is an automatic response out of your worried gadget, a few stressors arise at predictable times: your shuttle to work, a meeting along with your boss, or your own family gatherings, as an instance. While coping with such predictable stressors, you could both exchange the state of affairs or trade your reaction. While finding out which choice to choose in any given state of affairs, it's beneficial to think of the 4 A's: avoid, modify, adapt, or be given.

Earn how to mention "no." realize your limits and stick to them. Whether or not for your personal or professional lifestyles, taking up greater than you can take care of is a surefire recipe for pressure. Distinguish among the "should" and the "musts" and, while viable; say "no" to taking on too much.

Avoid people who stress you out. If a person continually causes stress in your lifestyles, limit the amount of time you spend with that man or woman or end the connection.

Take control of your environment. If the evening information makes you annoying, turn off the television. If visitors make you demanding, take an extended, less-traveled direction, however. If going to the marketplace is an unpleasant chore, do your grocery buying online.

Regulate the scenario

If you may keep away from a stressful scenario, try to modify it. Often, this involves changing the manner you speak and function for each day's existence.

Be inclined to compromise. While you ask someone to exchange their behavior, be inclined to do the equal. In case you each are willing to bend at the least a touch, you'll have a great hazard of finding a glad middle floor.

Create a balanced time table. All paintings and no play is a recipe for burnout. Try to discover a balance among work and circle of relative's life, social activities and solitary interests, day by day duties, and downtime.

Adapt to the stressor

If you can't exchange the stressor, trade yourself. You may adapt to demanding situations and regain your sense of manipulate by way of converting your expectancies and mind-set.

Reframe issues. Try to view disturbing situations from a greater superb perspective. In place of fuming approximately a traffic jam, observe it as an possibility to pause and regroup, pay attention to your favorite radio station, or experience a few on my own time.

Observe the huge picture. Take the attitude of the demanding situation. Ask yourself how vital it is going to be ultimately. Will it remember in a month? A year? Is it worth getting disillusioned over?

Adjust your requirements. Perfectionism is a primary source of avoidable stress. Prevent setting yourself up for failure by disturbing perfection. Set reasonable requirements for yourself and others, and discover ways to be okay with "precise sufficient."

Exercise gratitude. While stress is getting you down, take a moment to reflect on all the things you admire in your life, including your fantastic traits and gifts. This easy strategy will let you maintain things in perspective.

Take delivery of the matters you couldn't change

A few sources of pressure are unavoidable. You can't prevent or trade stressors along with the death of a cherished one, an extreme infection, or a countrywide recession. In such cases, a nice manner of coping with stress is to accept things as they may be simply. Acceptance may be difficult; however, in the long run, it's less complicated than railing against a situation you may change.

Don't attempt to manage the uncontrollable. Many stuff in life is beyond our manipulate, especially the behavior of other humans. Rather than stressing out over them, cognizance of the things you could control, including the manner you pick to react to problems.

Search for the upside. When going through primary challenges, try to examine them as opportunities for non-public increase.

In case your bad selections contributed to an annoying situation, reflect on them, and learn out of your errors.

Learn to forgive. Take delivery of the fact that we live in a less than excellent world and that human beings make mistakes. Let pass on anger and resentment. Free yourself from poor power with the aid of forgiving and transferring on.

Expressing what you're going via can be very cathartic, although there's not anything you may do to adjust the traumatic state of affairs. Communicate to a trusted pal or make an appointment with a therapist.

Tip three: Get transferring

When you're confused, the closing element you likely experience like doing is getting up and workout. But bodily interest is a big stress reliever—and you don't should be an athlete or spend hours in a gymnasium to enjoy the advantages. Workout releases endorphins that make you sense suitable, and it can additionally serve as a treasured distraction out of your each day's issues.

Placed on a few song and dance round

Take your canine for a walk

Walk or cycle to the grocery store

Use the stairs at domestic or work in preference to an elevator

Park your automobile within the farthest spot inside the lot and walk the relaxation of the way

Pair up with a workout companion and encourage every other as you work out

Play Ping-Pong or an pastime-primarily based video game together with your children

The stress-busting magic of mindful rhythmic workout

Even as pretty much any shape of physical pastime can help burn away anxiety and stress, rhythmic sports are mainly effective. Accurate selections include strolling, jogging, swimming, dancing, biking, tai chi, and aerobics. However, anything you pick, ensure its something you enjoy so that you're more likely to stay with it.

While you're exercising, make a conscious attempt to pay attention to your frame and the physical (and sometimes emotional) sensations you revel in as you're transferring. Cognizance on coordinating your respiration together with your actions, for example, or be aware of how the air or daylight feels in your pores and skin. Adding this mindfulness element will assist you break out of the cycle of negative thoughts that frequently accompany overwhelming pressure.

Tip four: connect with others

Young woman arms over face

There's not anything more calming than spending the best time with another individual who makes you sense safe and understood. In truth, face-to-face interaction triggers a cascade of hormones that counteracts the frame's defensive "combat-or-flight" reaction. It's nature's herbal stress reliever (as an brought bonus, it additionally enables stave off despair and anxiety). So make it a factor to connect regularly—and in character—with a circle of relatives and friends.

Remember that the human beings you talk to don't have that allows you to repair your stress. They honestly want to be properly listeners. And attempt no longer to allow concerns approximately looking vulnerable or being a burden maintains you from commencing up. The folks that care approximately you will be flattered by using your belief. It's going to simplest toughen your bond.

Of path, it's not continually realistic to have a friend close by to lean on while you feel overwhelmed using pressure, however using building and keeping a community of close buddies, you may improve your resiliency to life's stressors.

Tip five: find time for amusing and relaxation

Beyond a take-fee technique and a high-quality mindset, you may lessen stress for your lifestyles by carving out "me" time. Don't get so stuck up in the hustle and bustle of life which you neglect to attend to your very own needs. Nurturing yourself is a necessity, now not a luxurious. In case you regularly make time for fun and rest, you'll be in a better area to handle existence's stressors.

Set apart enjoyment time. Include relaxation and relaxation to your every day time table. Don't permit other duties to encroach. This is your time to take a ruin from all responsibilities and recharge your batteries.

Do something you enjoy each day. Make time for entertainment activities that carry you joy, whether it be stargazing, playing the piano, or working to your motorcycle.

Hold your humorousness. This consists of the ability to laugh at yourself. The act of guffawing facilitates your body combat stress in some of the approaches.

Take in a rest exercise. Rest strategies such as yoga, meditation, and deep breathing spark off the frame's rest reaction, a country of restfulness that is the alternative of the combat or flight or mobilization stress reaction. As you learn and exercise these strategies, your pressure tiers will lower, and your thoughts and body will become calm and targeted.

Tip 6: manage some time better

Terrible time control can purpose quite a few stress. When you're stretched too skinny and going for walks behind, it's difficult to stay calm and focused. Plus, you'll be tempted to keep away from or reduce back on all the healthful stuff you should be doing to preserve stress in tests, like socializing and getting sufficient sleep. The best news: there are matters you can do to attain healthier paintings-lifestyles stability.

Don't over-commit yourself. Keep away from scheduling things again-to-returned or seeking to match an excessive amount of into sooner or later. All too often, we underestimate how long things will take.

Prioritize responsibilities. Make a list of obligations you need to do and tackle them in order of significance. Do the high-precedence gadgets first. If you have something especially ugly or traumatic to do, get it over with early. The rest of your day can be extra great as a result.

Damage tasks into small steps. If a massive mission seems overwhelming, make a step-by using-step plan. Consciousness on one plausible step at a time, as opposed to taking on the whole lot immediately.

You don't have to do it all yourself, whether or not at home, college, or the job. If other people can take care of the undertaking, why not let them? Let pass the desire to manipulate or oversee each little step. You'll be letting move of useless stress within the method.

Tip 7: preserve stability with a healthy lifestyle

Pressure loose lady with earbuds in her ears

Similarly to ordinary exercise, there are other healthy lifestyle picks that could grow your resistance to stress.

Consume a healthy weight loss program. Properly-nourished, our bodies are better organized to address stress, so take into account what you devour. Begin your day proper with breakfast, and maintain your strength up and your mind clear with balanced, nutritious meals in the day.

Lessen caffeine and sugar. The temporary "highs" caffeine and sugar provide often lead to a crash in mood and electricity. Using reducing the amount of espresso, smooth liquids, chocolate, and sugary snacks to your weight loss plan, you'll sense more secure, and you'll sleep better.

Keep away from alcohol, cigarettes, and tablets. Self-medicating with alcohol or drugs may also offer a clean escape from stress. However, the comfort is the simplest transient. Don't keep away from or masks the difficulty to hand; deal with problems head-on and with clean thoughts.

Get sufficient sleep. Ok, sleep fuels your thoughts, in addition to your body. Feeling tired will increase your stress due to the fact it could reason you to suppose irrationally.

Tip 8: learn to relieve stress in the moment

While you're frazzled using your morning commute, caught in a worrying assembly at paintings, or fried from some other argument along with your spouse, you need a manner to manipulate your stress levels properly now. That's in which quick pressure relief comes in.

Chapter 2

Panic Attacks and Panic Disorder

Ever experienced a surprising surge of overwhelming tension and worry? Discover this guide to panic assaults, inclusive of signs and symptoms, remedy, and self-assist suggestions.

What's a panic attack?

A panic attack is a severe wave of fear characterized by its unexpectedness and debilitating, immobilizing intensity. Your heart kilos, you may breathe, and you may feel like you're dying or going loopy. Panic often attacks strikeout of the blue, without any caution, and occasionally without a clean trigger. They'll even occur while you're cozy or asleep.

A panic assault can be a one-time incidence, even though many human beings enjoy repeat episodes. Recurrent panic attacks are often brought on by way of a specific scenario, along with crossing a bridge or talking in public—mainly if that scenario has brought about a panic assault earlier than. Generally, the panic-inducing situation is one in that you sense endangered and not able to break out, triggering the body's combat-or-flight reaction.

You can experience one or greater panic attacks, yet be otherwise perfectly happy and healthy. Or your panic attacks might also arise as a part of some other disorder, together with panic sickness, social phobia, or melancholy. Regardless of the cause, panic attacks are treatable. There are techniques you can use to lessen or eliminate the signs and symptoms of panic, regain your self-assurance, and take control of your life again.

Paula's story

Paula had her first panic attack six months in the past. She became in her workplace getting ready for a critical paintings presentation when, abruptly, she felt a severe wave of fear. Then the room started spinning, and he or she felt like she turned into going to throw up. Her whole frame was shaking, she couldn't catch her breath, and her heart changed into pounding out of her chest. She gripped her table until the episode handed, but it left her deeply shaken.

Paula had her subsequent panic attack three weeks later, and in view that then, they've been happening with growing frequency. She is no way is aware of while or wherein she'll go through an assault, but she's afraid of having one in public.

Consequently, she's been staying home after work, rather than going out with pals. She also refuses to ride the elevator as much as her 12th ground workplace out of worry of being trapped if she has a panic attack.

Panic attack signs and symptoms

The symptoms and signs and symptoms of a panic assault increase all of a sudden and typically attain their height inside 10 minutes. They rarely last greater than an hour, with maximum finishing inside 20 to half-hour. Panic assaults can occur everywhere and at any time. You may have one even as you're in a shop purchasing, taking walks down the street, using for your automobile, or maybe sitting on the sofa at home.

Panic attack signs and symptoms encompass:

Shortness of breath or hyperventilation

Coronary heart palpitations or racing heart

Chest pain or soreness

Trembling or shaking

Choking feeling

Feeling unreal or detached out of your surroundings

Sweating

Nausea or disillusioned stomach

Feeling dizzy, light-headed, or faint

Numbness or tingling sensations

Warm or cold flashes

Worry of demise, losing manage, or going crazy

Is it a heart attack or a panic assault?

Maximum of the symptoms of a panic assault are bodily, and generally, these symptoms are so extreme that you may think you have a heart assault. Many human beings laid low with panic attacks make repeated trips to the health practitioner or the emergency room in an attempt to get remedy for what they agree with is a lifestyles-threatening medical trouble. Even as it's essential to rule out possible medical reasons for symptoms consisting of chest ache, increased coronary heart fee, or trouble respiratory, it's often panic. This is overlooked as a capacity cause—not the alternative manner round.

Signs and signs and symptoms of panic ailment

While many human beings revel in just one or panic attacks without similar episodes of headaches—and there's little purpose to fear if that's you—a few people cross on to increase panic ailment. Panic disorder is characterized by the aid of repeated panic assaults, combined with fundamental changes in behavior or persistent tension over having also assaults.

You will be suffering from panic disease in case you:

Enjoy common, unexpected panic assaults that aren't tied to a specific state of affairs

Worry plenty approximately having some other panic attack

Are behaving in another way due to the panic attacks, inclusive of fending off places in which you've previously panicked

While a single panic assault may additionally best closing a couple of minutes, the results of the experience can go away a lasting imprint. If you have panic ailment, the recurrent panic assaults take an emotional toll. The reminiscence of the extreme worry and terror which you felt at some stage in the assaults can negatively impact yourself-self-belief and purpose extreme disruption in your everyday lifestyles. Subsequently, this results in the following panic sickness signs:

Anticipatory tension – instead of feeling secure and like your everyday self in among panic attacks, you experience disturbing and tense. This anxiety stems from a fear of getting destiny panic attacks. This "fear of fear" is a gift most of the time and can be extremely disabling.

Phobic avoidance – You begin to avoid certain situations or environments. This avoidance can be primarily based on the notion that the state of affairs you're averting brought about a previous panic assault. Or you may keep away from places where break out could be hard or assist might be unavailable if you had a panic attack. Taken to its extreme, phobic avoidance becomes agoraphobia.

Panic disease with agoraphobia

Agoraphobia becomes traditionally thought to involve a worry of public places and open spaces. However, it's far now believed that agoraphobia develops as a problem of panic assaults and panic disease. Although it could develop at any point, agoraphobia normally seems inside a year of your first recurrent panic attacks.

If you're agoraphobic, you're afraid of getting a panic attack in a situation wherein break out would be hard or embarrassing. You may additionally be afraid of having a panic attack wherein you wouldn't be capable of getting assistance. Because of these fears, you start keeping off increasingly more conditions.

As an example, you could begin to avoid:

Crowded places inclusive of purchasing shops or sports arenas.

Social gatherings, eating places, or different situations in which it would be embarrassing to have a panic attack.

Physical exercising in case it triggers panic.

Positive food or beverages that might provoke panic, which include alcohol, caffeine, sugar, or specific medicines.

You are going everywhere without the company of someone who makes you experience secure. In more extreme instances, you might handiest feel safe at domestic.

Reasons for panic attacks and panic sickness

Even though the precise causes of panic assaults and panic disease are doubtful, the tendency to have panic assaults runs in families. There also seems to be a connection with predominant lifestyles transitions such as graduating from college and entering the place of business, getting married, or having a toddler. Severe stress, consisting of the death of a cherished one, divorce, or activity loss, also can cause panic attacks.

Panic assaults also can be due to scientific situations and other bodily reasons. In case you're suffering from signs and symptoms of panic, it's important to look a health practitioner to rule out the subsequent opportunities:

Mitral valve prolapse, a minor cardiac trouble that happens when one of the coronary heart's valves doesn't close efficaciously

Hyperthyroidism (overactive thyroid gland)

Hypoglycemia (low blood sugar)

Stimulant use (amphetamines, cocaine, caffeine)

Medicinal drug withdrawal

Self-assist recommendations for panic attacks

Girl enjoyable in chair regardless of how powerless or out of manage you can sense about your panic assaults, it's important to realize that there are many matters you may do to help yourself. The following self-help strategies can make a big difference in helping you overcome panic:

Learn about panic and tension. Knowing greater about panic can pass an extended way towards relieving your misery. Read up on anxiety, panic sickness, and the fight-or-flight response experienced during a panic assault. You'll learn that the sensations and emotions you have while you panic are ordinary and that you aren't going loopy.

Avoid smoking, alcohol, and caffeine. Those can all initiate panic attacks in prone people. In case you need assistance to kick the cigarette dependancy, see a way to Stop Smoking. Also, be careful with medicinal drugs that incorporate stimulants, along with weight loss program drugs and non-drowsy bloodless medications.

Learn how to control your respiration. Hyperventilation brings on many sensations (including lightheadedness and tightness of the chest) that arise all through a panic assault. Deep respiration, then again, can relieve the symptoms of panic. By way of learning to manipulate your respiratory, you may calm yourself down while you begin to experience demanding. And if you recognize the way to control your respiratory, you're also less possible to create the very sensations which you're terrified of.

Exercise relaxation strategies. While practiced often, activities along with yoga, meditation, and progressive muscle relaxation support the frame's rest reaction—the other of the pressure response worried in anxiety and panic. And not only do those rest practices sell relaxation, but they also increase emotions of pleasure and serenity.

Join face-to-face with a circle of relatives and friends. Symptoms of tension can emerge as worse when you feel isolated, so attain out to those who care about you on an ordinary basis. In case you feel that you don't have all of us to show to, explore ways to satisfy new human beings and build supportive friendships.

You are exercising regularly. Exercise is a natural tension reliever, so try and get transferring for at least half-hour on most days (3 10-minute periods is just as suitable). Rhythmic aerobic workout that requires moving both your arms and legs—like walking, walking, swimming, or dancing—may be in particular effective.

Get enough restful sleep. Inadequate or poor first-class sleep can make anxiety worse, so try to get seven to nine hours of restful sleep a night. If slumbering nicely is a hassle for you, these suggestions to getting a great night's sleep can assist.

Remedy for panic attacks and panic ailment

Girl on couch in remedy the only form of professional treatment for tackling panic attacks, panic sickness, and agoraphobia is remedy. Even a quick route of remedy can help.

Cognitive-behavioral therapy makes a specialty of the questioning styles and behaviors which are sustaining or triggering your panic assaults and helps you study your fears in a more sensible light. For example, if you had a panic assault at the same time as driving, what's the worst factor that would genuinely happen? While you might have to pull over to the aspect of the road, you are not possible to crash your car or have a heart assault. After you study that not anything genuinely disastrous is going to show up, the experience of panic will become much less terrifying.

Exposure therapy for panic disease lets in you to revel in the bodily sensations of panic in a safe and controlled environment, supplying you with the opportunity to learn more healthy methods of coping. You will be asked to hyperventilate, shake your head to and fro, or maintain your breath. Those distinctive sporting events cause sensations, much like the symptoms of panic. With every publicity, you grow to be less afraid of those inner physical sensations and experience a greater sense of manage over your panic.

Exposure remedy for panic disease with agoraphobia includes exposure to the conditions you worry and avoid is likewise included in remedy. As in exposure therapy for precise phobias, you face the scary state of affairs till the panic begins to move away. Via this revel in, you analyze that the state of affairs isn't dangerous and that you have manage over your emotions.

Medication for panic attacks and panic disorder

Medicinal drugs can be used to briefly manage or lessen some of the signs of panic sickness. But, it doesn't treat or solve the hassle. Medicinal drugs can be useful in intense instances;

however, it ought to not be the only treatment pursued. Medication is simplest while mixed with different remedies, such as remedy and way of life adjustments that cope with the underlying causes of panic disorder.

Medicinal drugs used can also consist of:

Anti-depressants. It takes numerous weeks earlier than they begin to work, so that you ought to take them constantly, no longer simply for the duration of a panic attack.

Benzodiazepines. These are anti-tension drugs that act in no time (commonly within a half-hour to an hour). Taking them for the duration of a panic assault affords rapid alleviation of signs and symptoms. But, benzodiazepines are quite addictive and have serious withdrawal signs, so they ought to be used with warning.

The way to assist a person having a panic attack
Seeing a friend or loved one suffering a panic attack may be scary. Their respiratory may additionally end up abnormally speedy and shallow; they may end up dizzy or mild-headed,

tremble, sweat, experience nausea, or suppose they have a heart attack. No matter how irrational you believe, you studied their panicked reaction to a situation is, it's critical to understand that the hazard appears very actual to the one that you love. Surely telling them to calm down or minimizing their worry received help. However, by way of supporting your loved one ride out a panic attack, you can help them feel less terrified of any destiny attacks.

Stay calms you. Being calm, understanding, and non-judgmental will assist your loved ones' panic subsides quicker.

Awareness the one you love on their respiration. Find a quiet region to your friend to sit down and then guide them to take gradual, deep breaths for a few minutes.

Do something physical. Collectively, increase and decrease your hands or stamp your ft. It can help to burn off a number of your beloved's stress.

Get your buddy out in their head by way of asking them to name five matters around them or talking soothingly about a shared hobby.

Encourage the one that you love to are seeking help. As soon as the panic attack is over, the one you love might also feel embarrassed approximately having an assault in front of you. Reassure them and encourage them to are trying to find help for their tension.

The important thing to Overcoming Panic attacks

The optimum direction to overcoming panic assaults is to educate you to respond to panic in accepting and calming ways.

This text will display you a specific, simple, and powerful set of guidelines for overcoming panic attacks. This material comes from my Panic attacks Workbook.

If you pick paying attention to studying, here is a radio interview in which I speak those steps.

As you examine the steps defined underneath, think about how they compare to what you typically do all through a panic assault. The Panic Trick tells us that your intestine intuition of the way to reply to a panic assault will probably be to do something that makes the problem worse in preference to better. The route to overcoming panic attacks requires responses that are pretty exceptional from what you commonly do. In case you maintain doing the equal issue, you may, in all likelihood, maintain getting equal results. In case you are seeking anxiety alleviation, you need to look for one of a kind strategies.

You can use these five steps to manual your responses at some point of a panic attack. The normal use of this technique will pass an extended way closer to your intention of overcoming panic assaults. I've tailored them, with a few changes of my personal, from tension issues and Phobias: A Cognitive attitude, an amazing professional textual content by way of Beck, Greenberg, and Emery.

The 5 Steps of aware

The five steps to overcoming panic attacks are:

Acknowledge & be given

Wait & Watch (and perhaps, work)

Moves (to make myself more cozy)

Repeat

End

Allows test what each step entails.

Renowned & accept

All development starts right here. This is the maximum critical single step to overcoming panic assaults.

Renowned

Right here, I acknowledge the present truth, that I'm afraid and starting to panic. I won't try and ignore it, or pretend it's not there. I won't warfare to distract myself, inform myself to "forestall thinking about it!" or snap any rubber bands on my wrist.

I'm acknowledging simply that I am afraid, not that I'm in hazard. The notion that I'm in threat is simply every other symptom of panic, not a critical or useful idea.

Be given

Right here, I receive the reality that I am afraid at this second. I do not fight the sensation; ask God to take it away; blame myself, or every person else. I will be given, as first-rate I can, that I am afraid in the same way I might receive a headache. I don't like headaches, but I don't bang my head towards the wall to remove them, because that makes them worse. Overcoming panic attacks starts with operating with, no longer towards, my panic and anxiety signs.

How can I be given a Panic attack?

What makes a panic assault applicable (no longer perfect, however proper) is that, while it feels lousy and fills me with dread, it isn't risky. It may not kill me or make me loopy. Someone pointing a gun at me, it is no longer proper. I'd get hurt or killed. If a person factors a gun at me, I must do anything I will to trade that: run, cover, fight, yell, bribe, or beg, because the consequence of being shot is so terrible that I must attempt to avoid it.

On the other hand - a policeman giving me a price tag, although I don't deserve it, I can live with that, and may hopefully keep my temper in check, so I don't make matters worse for myself.

Accepting the signs, now not resisting, is an effective step to overcoming panic attacks.

What Can a Panic attack do to me?

It makes me experience afraid; that is what a panic attack does. And, if I have a panic assault, I'm already there! I am already experiencing the worst on the way to appear. I just want to trip it out. This is the standard gold route to overcoming panic assaults.

Why should I take delivery of a panic attack? Because the extra I face up to panic, the more dangerous it receives. The extra I increase the habit of recognition, the more excellent development I make toward my goal of overcoming panic assaults.

It truly is renowned & takes delivery of. How does that examine to what you usually do throughout a panic assault?

Wait & Watch (and maybe, paintings)

Wait

What I suggest by "Wait" is this: don't simply do something, stand there. It is just like the proposal, "remember to 10 before you get mad".

One of the hallmarks of a panic assault is that it temporarily robs you of your capacity to think, consider, and concentrate.

This step will purchase you a touch time to regain those capabilities earlier than you take any motion.

When you react before you have got a risk to assume instantly, what do you do? If you are like most of the people, you probably flee or struggle. You do things that truly make it worse. This is what humans meanwhile, they are saying things like, "I understand I'm doing it to myself," and the more difficult I try, the worse it gets.

Jumping into action too fast is a big impediment to overcoming panic attacks.

So, even though you've got an effective urge to depart, delay that choice for a little bit. Don't tell yourself you cannot depart - preserve that option open so you don't feel trapped - but take away the decision approximately whether or not or no longer to depart. Live inside the scenario. You don't want to run away to get comfort. Permit alleviation comes to you.

Watch

Use the occasion to look at how the panic works, and how you respond to it. The high-quality manner of doing that is to fill out a panic diary. The diary is a questionnaire that allows you to notice vital aspects of a panic attack so that you can reply greater efficiently over the years. Feel loose to download and reproduce it in your personal use. You may also download hard and fast commands.

My sufferers regularly record that just filling out a diary allows them to relax. How do these paintings? It is now not that they're distracted from the problem of panic, because the diary questions are all approximately panic. It helps you get a little distance out of your emotions. It works due to the fact, even as you complete a diary, you're within the function of an observer, in preference to feeling like a victim.

The fine way to use the diary is to fill it out for the duration of the attack, rather than after. If you're in a scenario wherein writing is impractical, possibly at the same time as riding a car, you can: use a virtual recorder; have your assist person examine the inquiries to you and record your answers; or pull over for a couple of minutes to put in writing.

What about "work"?

In case you're in a surprisingly passive scenario at some point in the panic attack - a passenger in a vehicle, getting your hair cut, or waiting in a ready room - "Wait & Watch" is all you need. In case you're in a more active role - riding an automobile or giving a presentation - you then also need to take care of the "paintings" of accomplishing that hobby. Do "Wait & Watch," but also stay engaged for your project.

It is "Wait & Watch (and maybe, paintings)." How does that evaluate to what you commonly do during a panic assault?

Actions (to make myself greater cozy)

At this point, you've already gone via the two maximum critical steps to overcoming panic assaults.

Those steps, and all of the steps vital to conquer panic ailment and phobia, are included in plenty more detail in my Panic attacks Workbook.

What's your task for the duration of an attack?

It is not your activity to deliver the panic attack to a stop; to be able to take place regardless of what you do. Do not take my word for it. Review your records with panic assaults. Have you ever had one that failed to end?

The truth is, each panic attack ends irrespective of what you do. If you respond inside the most compelling manner feasible and do an awesome job at bringing it in for a soft touchdown, that panic assault will end. And if you do the entirety, the maximum unhelpful way feasible - suffering and resisting and fleeing in approaches that make the panic worse - which one will end also. Even the primary panic assault a person has after they have the least concept of what is taking place, those cease as well.

The cease of a panic attack is a part of a panic attack, simply as a good deal as the start of 1 is a part of it. It is no longer something you need to supply or make manifest. The panic assault will stop irrespective of what you do. Even while you don't trust it'll end, if you have the nervous thoughts that it's going to ultimate forever, it nonetheless ends.

So what is your job throughout a panic attack? It is an extra modest assignment than you probably meant. Your task is to look if you could make your self a little greater secure while you look forward to the attack to give up. And in case you cannot even make yourself a bit greater comfy, then your process is to watch for it to end.

Here are some techniques that my sufferers have discovered, especially beneficial at the same time as waiting for an attack to end.

Stomach respiratory

No matter what else you do, do belly breathing. It is also known as diaphragmatic breathing, but I assume "stomach respiration" is more descriptive. Many humans suppose they know how to do deep respiratory; however, do not do it efficiently so that they do not get good effects. A good belly respiration approach is a completely powerful device within the work of overcoming panic attacks!

How to talk to your self

Communicate to yourself (silently!) approximately what is going on, and what you want to do. One query my patients find very useful is this: is it hazard or soreness? Some of the opposite responses my patients like encompass the subsequent:

1. Exceptional allows having an attack! It's a terrific risk to exercise my coping techniques.

2. Answer "what if...?" fears by announcing, "So what? I'll get afraid, then loosen up once more."

3. It's ok to be afraid.

Get involved within the gift

People don't panic within the present. People panic after they believe something terrible going on to them in destiny or inside the beyond. This is why your panic attacks are almost usually followed via a few "what if...?" concept. The reason you are saying "what if...?" what you worry is due to the fact it is not going on!

Get returned into the pastime you were engaged in previous to the assault, and emerge as involved with the human beings and gadgets around you. In case you're in a store, resume shopping, reading labels, comparing costs, asking questions, and so on. It's going to circulate you closer to your aim of overcoming panic assaults while you convey your recognition and power again to the existing environment. By this I mean, paintings with what is around you.

Work with Your Body

Become aware of, and loosen up, the elements of your frame that get most stressful during a panic attack. This generally involves first tensing, after which enjoyable, the muscle groups of your jaw, neck, shoulders, returned, and legs. Do no longer permit yourself to face inflexible, muscle mass tensed, and protecting your breath. That makes you sense worse! In case you feel such as you "can't flow a muscle," start with just one finger!

It is "movements (to make myself more secure)." How does that compare with what you usually do for the duration of a panic attack?

Repeat

This step is right here due to the fact you might start feeling higher, then feel every other wave of panic. Your first response may then be to suppose, "Oh No, it failed to work!". The Repeat step is here to remind you that it's good enough if that occurs. Take it from the top once more. It is not unusual or risky. You could go through numerous cycles, and also you simply want to repeat the conscious steps once more, as frequently as you need.

How does that evaluate what you generally do?

Cease

This is right here to remind you that your panic attack will end; that each one panic attacks end; that they give up irrespective of the way you reply; that it is no longer your activity to make the attack cease; and that your simplest activity is to make yourself as secure as feasible while looking forward to the attack to cease.

Have those statements been real for you? Don't take my word for it — assessment your records of panic attacks and notice.

Overcoming Panic attacks

It will take you through the stairs, from A to Z, of the way to cope with panic assaults in ways that lead them to vanish away, in addition to how to conquer the phobias and avoidance that commonly accompany panic.

How to prevent a Panic attack

That's a phrase we hear countless times in a day. We pay attention to it in communication, on television, within the films. We are saying it to ourselves. Why? Due to the fact when we panic– revel in an extreme sensation of worry or anxiety in reaction to a real threat—we are more likely to lose manage and react to probably hazardous, even life-threatening occasions frantically or irrationally. Panic inhibits our ability to reason, really or logically. Consider the explosion of worry, the borderline hysteria you felt the day you momentarily overlooked your six-year-old in the mall. Or the time your vehicle skidded violently on a rain-soaked avenue. Even earlier than you registered what became going on, your body launched adrenaline, cortisol, and other hormones that signal danger. The ones hormones cause physical reactions: heart-pounding, shallow respiration, sweating and shivering, shaking, and different ugly bodily sensations.

Sooner or later in our lives, most folks will experience a panic assault in reaction to a real threat or acute pressure. However, while panic assaults arise or recur for no cause and in the absence of risk or extreme stress, or when the concern of experiencing another attack is so robust which you change your conduct with the aid of avoiding sure places or human beings, you can have panic disorder.

The give up of the whole thing: What a Panic attack seems like

Only 16, Caroline had her first panic assault a year in the past. Her mother changed into losing her off at her summertime activity at a neighborhood faculty while, without warning, a full-blown panic assault engulfed her. "My coronary heart began racing, and my body felt so warm. I started to sweat and shake uncontrollably. My vision became distorted, and my frame felt limp, like a moist noodle," she says. For 20 mins, till the panic attacked passed, Caroline refused to get out of the auto. Her mother didn't recognize what to do.

Throughout the day, if she was out, the assault felt "like my head weighed a thousand pounds, and my chest might get truly heavy. It actually felt like something became pulling me down. I generally ought to head home right away. I'd then experience foggy vision in which it ...honestly looked like there was fog inside the air. I also skilled double imaginative and prescient and components of my frame—like my neck or one arm or one complete facet of my face– could go definitely numb."

Emotional turmoil and the physical manifestations that Caroline and Kirstie describe panic assaults can purpose palpitations, pounding coronary heart or improved coronary heart price; sweating; trembling or shaking; sensations of shortness of breath or smothering; emotions of choking; chest pain or discomfort; nausea or stomach distress; feeling dizzy, unsteady, mild-headed or faint; chills or overheating; numbness or tingling; feelings of unreality (derealization) or being detached from oneself (depersonalization); fear of losing manage or "going loopy"; and worry of demise.

Remote attacks are terrible enough. However, whilst the attacks recur in a quick time period, or while the concern of another assault is so strong which you begin to keep away from situations, places, and people that could trigger an assault, you may be identified with panic ailment.

Preventing Panic: What to do whilst you have a Panic assault

Here, some strategies which have worked for others which can help you:

1) Deep respiratory: enjoyable your frame can help evade an anxiety attack. Practice breathing in through your nose for a remember of 5, maintain it for five after which breath out via mouth for a matter of 5. Or take a class in meditation and respiratory strategies

2) in case you all of a sudden feel your coronary heart pounding or enjoy different bodily clues that an anxiety attack is barreling for you, do that distraction cautioned through Rob Cole, LHMC, medical director of mental fitness offerings at Banyan remedy facilities. Begin counting backward from 100 with the aid of 3s. The act of counting at random periods helps you to recognize and overrides the annoying mind which might be looking to sneak into your psyche. Better still maintain loose exchange in your pocket. Upload a dime to a nickel, and then add pennies and so forth. By means of controlling your thoughts and that specialize in something outside yourself, you may be to experience calmer.

Three) Grounding your self is another useful technique. Track yourself into four things around you that you could see, three matters you can contact, two which you odor, and one you may flavor. Again, forcing your mind to remember something outside yourself allows, says Cole.

4) Ice, Ice child. For nighttime panic attacks, Kirstie Craine Ruiz continues about four equipped-to-go ice packs—2 big and a pair of small– in her freezer. While she feels panic coming she puts two small ones in her hand and the two large ones on my decrease again. "if your coronary heart is actually racing and your respiratory is horrific, I would advise taking the one in your belly and rubbing it from the middle of your chest all the way down to the bottom of your belly, slowly, and again and again, till your coronary heart charge begins to mellow (over your shirt, of course- you don't want to make your self freezing!). I sense like after I do that, it literally actions the hyper electricity down from my chest and alleviates any chest pain. This approach constantly allows me while it feels like my heart is in my throat. When you feel as even though you can breathe again, place the packs on your decrease stomach or lower back, and inside the palms of your fingers. I don't know if it's stress points but holding small smooth ice packs in each arms with arms up, does wonders for my panic, to at the moment."

5) Caroline, 16, has discovered dialectical behavior therapy helpful, and she's observed that her panic attacks can be heightened if no longer precipitated by means of shiny mild. Her tip: wear sunglasses. She additionally shies away from conversation at some stage in the assault. "Don't question me if I'm ok," she says.

Who receives Panic attacks?

At least 6 million Americans are afflicted by panic assaults and panic sickness, each condition categorized as anxiety problems. According to the anxiety and melancholy affiliation of us (ADAA), about 2-3% of Americans enjoy panic disease in a given 12 months, and it's far two times as not unusual in women as in men. Panic sickness commonly affects people when they're in their 20s but is likewise visible in younger children, teens, and older adults.

What reasons Panic disease?

At the same time, as the precise reasons are not recognized, what researchers do recognize is that panic disorder does occasionally run in families. And it's miles regularly visible in those who be afflicted by different anxiety problems explains Cole.

As an instance, someone with obsessive-compulsive ailment may additionally revel in a panic attack while their time table or compulsions are interrupted. People who warfare with unique phobias also are liable to panic attacks. Someone with an intense worry of heights (acrophobia) might also experience a panic assault in a penthouse rental. And for someone with generalized tension disease (GAD), a situation characterized through extreme worry or fear, and the endless anxiety can strengthen to a panic assault. Human beings with put up-demanding stress disorder (PTSD) have a higher occurrence of panic sickness than the overall population. Infection or stressful occasions increase the possibilities of panic attacks.

Human beings with hyperthyroidism (Graves' disease), mitral valve prolapse, and other situations or sicknesses also may be extra without problems precipitated.

Treatment options
Panic assaults and panic sickness are treatable as soon as the underlying cause of is diagnosed. "typically clinical conditions

and other factors (substance use or withdrawal from materials) are ruled out earlier than making the analysis," says Flo Leighton, psychiatric nurse practitioner, and therapist with Union square exercise in new york. Getting to the foundation reason typically takes a couple of periods, says Leighton. Here are a few alternatives that may be endorsed to you :

Cognitive-behavioral therapy (CBT) is based totally on the concept that our thoughts cause our feelings and behaviors, not outside things, like humans, conditions, and activities. In keeping with the countrywide association of Cognitive Behavioral Therapists, the benefit of this therapy is that we can change the manner we suppose to sense and act higher despite the fact that the situation does no longer alternate. CBT makes a specialty of determining the idea and conduct styles liable for maintaining or causing the panic assaults. CBT is a time-stressed technique (treatment dreams—and the range of periods anticipated to gain them—are established at the start) that employs a ramification of cognitive and behavioral strategies to affect trade.

Dialectical behavior remedy (DBT) is the shape of Cognitive remedy that emphasizes man or woman psychotherapy in addition to group skills training to help people learns new capabilities and strategies—consisting of mindfulness and distress tolerance– to manage their anxiety and panic. According to the American dental association therapists who practicing DBT aim to strike a stability among validation and alternate by way of absolutely communicating acceptance of who the consumer is and the demanding situations the client faces, at the same time as on the identical time assisting the consumer in analyzing new abilities to enhance emotion regulation, interpersonal communication abilities and the way to participate in existence and cope with problems without defaulting to impulsive behavior.

Typical, the first-class treatment entails a combination of treatments along with mindfulness, learning deep respiration strategies, yoga, and exercise.

Panic attacks: How do I stop them?

A panic attack is an unexpected feeling of severe worry or disabling tension. It may bring about such acute misery that someone fears they're losing manipulate or demise.

Understanding how to save you feelings of panic from spiraling out of management is an essential skill for folks that enjoy panic signs.

Situations, together with pressure and tension, can lead to panic assaults. Heart situations and blood disorders consisting of anemia, can purpose similar signs.

The depth of the assault normally peaks at around 10 minutes; however, symptoms can persist beyond that. A panic attack commonly occurs without caution and can be unrelated to any real chance or apparent purpose. They will even wake someone from a sound sleep.

Speedy statistics on anxiety attacks

Panic attacks are an overreaction by the amygdala or the concerned middle of the mind

Signs encompass a racing heart, sweating, issue catching breath, and a feeling of drawing close death or doom.

Twice as many women than men enjoy panic attacks.

Getting ready, calm respiration strategies, and mindfulness strategies can assist in holding panic assaults at bay.

Symptoms

Panic assaults can motive an experience of forthcoming doom, but they may be effortlessly treatable.

To forestall a panic attack, a person first wishes to understand the signs and symptoms and warning signs and symptoms.

A panic assault will cause as a minimum four of the signs and symptoms underneath:

A pounding, racing heart

Sweating

Shaking

Shortness of breath

Choking sensation

Chest soreness

Nausea

Dizzy, feeling faint

Feelings of unreality or detachment

Tingling or numbness

Chills or heat sensations

Worry of dropping sanity

Fear of dying

There isn't always constantly a clean pattern to panic attacks. A few human beings may additionally enjoy numerous assaults in an afternoon and then go months without another. Others may additionally have attacks on a weekly foundation.

However, a pattern may be identified. In situations together with agoraphobia or fear that being in public locations might also trigger a panic assault, human beings have the pattern of averting public locations.

Panic assaults can mimic different fitness situations. Anybody experiencing these signs must be evaluated through a healthcare professional to decide if there is an underlying medical reason.

Certain coronary heart issues, respiratory situations, overactive thyroid glands, and stimulants, including caffeine, can all motive similar signs.

Causes

The purpose of panic attacks is not completely understood, but research indicates that a mixture of genetic, organic, psychological, and environmental elements could make a person more susceptible to panic.

For instance, panic attacks may be resulting from brain biology that is over-sensitive to a worry stimulus or an over-reactive worry middle of the mind, and a structure referred to as the amygdala.

A panic attack takes place when the frame reports unexpected surge adrenaline out of percentage to any perceived threat or threat.

At some point in a panic assault, the amygdala reacts with a high-stress response while exposed to an unexpected scenario or after facing an annoying life event.

Panic attacks are as a result of the emotional middle of the brain overreacting to stimuli.

Adrenaline is the hormone involved inside the fight-or-flight reaction. An unexpected launch of this hormone prepares the frame to flee from or bodily confront chance by means of increasing the coronary heart and breathing rates, among other matters.

When the nervous system reacts in an ordinary way to a frightening scenario, adrenaline ranges speedy drop back to their normal tiers as soon as the supply of worry is eliminated. This does not show up with a panic attack, and a person may take an hour or extra to recover completely from the signs and symptoms.

Frequently there is no apparent trigger for the panic symptoms. This may motive human beings to try an explanation of the revel in with thoughts such as, "I ought to be death," or "I'm losing my mind." these minds can result in similarly panic signs.

A panic attack can also be brought about through an intimidating occasion, including public talking or flying.

The way to manipulate a panic attack

The coolest news approximately panic assault symptoms is that they may be extraordinarily treatable. There are many incredible ways for humans to self-manipulate panic reactions.

Education

Knowledge is a big part of overcoming panic attack signs. Learning about the way the worry center of the mind works can empower humans to recognize a panic assault for what it's miles: A misfiring of the amygdala causing a surge of adrenaline.

It is essential to keep in mind that the signs of panic aren't related to a severe illness. No matter the feelings of terror and experience of imminent doom, an assault will no longer lead to demise.

Understanding this could divert one's worrisome mind that could make an attack worse.

Calm breathing

Taking control of the respiratory is the first step to controlling a panic assault. The intention is to create a gradual move of air via breathing in and out. This prevents hyperventilation and a buildup of carbon dioxide inside the blood.

It is helpful to practice aware respiratory outside of panic attacks. This equips folks who experience panic assaults with the techniques designed to forestall them.

To practice calm respiration:

Take sluggish, regular breaths in through your nose, after which out through slightly puckered lips.

Breathe in for the count number of 5, hold for 1 second, and then exhale slowly to the remember of four.

Pause for two seconds, after which recap.

Repeat this for several cycles, or until you experience the frame, begin to relax.

Muscle rest

Any other beneficial approach is studying to loosen up the frame.

Tighten the muscle whilst taking a deep breath in, keep for some seconds, and then launch the anxiety while breathing out. Circulate up the frame, one muscle organization at a time.

Mindfulness and cognitive-behavioral remedy

Calm breathing can help to reduce overreactions inside the mind.

Mindfulness is the act of accepting thoughts as they arrive, however not letting them blow out of share. It's far an intellectual framework designed to help people live gifts inside the second without overanalyzing the worrying factors of existence.

Mindfulness contains many rest and meditation strategies.

Panic assaults can originate from the mind that spiral into deep-seated worries. Cognitive behavior remedy (CBT) is a powerful, lasting remedy for controlling panic attack signs and symptoms.

CBT is a useful choice for people who experience repeated panic assaults. CBT is demanding situations, anxious thoughts. What are you afraid will take place? Is there evidence to support those fears? A practitioner educated in CBT can equip an individual with the gear to effectively manipulate and defuse a full-blown panic attack.

Exercising

Everyday workout is important for retaining suitable fitness and should be integrated into day by day lifestyles. From community walks to aggressive sports, finding a hobby of hobby is critical. Exercise allows with stress management and encourages the body to produces herbal chemical compounds known as endorphins, which can be vital for ache remedy and a sense of properly-being.

Regular exercise in social placing can also assist improve someone's confidence and sense of community. This will reduce destiny triggers for panic attacks and foster a supportive network of folks who can assist if a panic attack does occur.

Planning beforehand

Making ready for recognized triggers and worrying conditions may be helpful.

What's it about the situation that causes emotions of terror? If it's far flying, as an example, speak to a pal who likes to fly and ask what they enjoy about it. Perhaps they are searching for reassurance from a flight attendant.

Different techniques that many people discover beneficial encompass:

Dressing in layers or wearing a portable fan to keep away from overheating

Having water accessible to maintain hydrated and cool

Internalizing reassuring statements or mantras, inclusive of "I'm secure," "I'm able to cope with this," or "This too shall skip."

Consume a wholesome weight-reduction plan

Consuming normal meals can assist preserve normal blood sugar degrees. Low blood sugar stages can make a contribution to panic signs and symptoms. A healthy weight-reduction plan includes:

By no means going extra than 4 hours without ingesting

Correcting any nutritional deficiencies

Keeping off caffeine and alcohol as they could cause or worsen panic assaults

Rule out underlying causes

Go to a health practitioner for a checkup to cope with any potential clinical problems. Anemia, allergies, and a few heart situations can cause panic attacks.

In case you discover it difficult to visit a doctor, deliver a chum or family member for help, and make certain to discover a personable, expert, and encouraging circle of relatives' physician.

Any smokers who revel in panic assaults ought to stop smoking as it's miles a contributor to panic. It may sense like smoking calms feelings of tension, but nicotine is a stimulant and may make lengthy-term tension worse.

Complementary and opportunity medicine

There may be a developing hobby in using opportunity medication interventions in the U.S. For both medical and anxiety associated disorders. Acupuncture, aromatherapy, and a few herbs may be a powerful, beneficial extra approach to controlling panic.

Medicinal drug

Medication should not be used as preliminary control for panic attack symptoms. If all other measures have now not helped, some tablets have been a hit in controlling panic assaults. Those include benzodiazepines and selective serotonin uptake inhibitors (SSRIs).

Ways to Stop a Panic Attack

Panic attacks

Panic assaults are sudden, extreme surges of worry, panic, or tension. They're overwhelming, and they have bodily as well as emotional signs.

Many people with panic assaults may additionally have issues respiratory, sweat profusely, tremble, and sense their hearts pounding.

Some humans will also enjoy chest pain and a feeling of detachment from truth or themselves throughout a panic assault, in order that they make think they have a heart assault. Others have reported feeling like they're having a stroke.

Panic attacks may be horrifying and may hit you fast. Right here are eleven strategies you could use to try and stop a panic attack when you're having one or when you experience one approach:

1. Use deep respiration

Even as hyperventilating is a symptom of panic assaults that may boom fear, deep respiration can lessen signs of panic during an attack.

If you're able to manipulate your breathing, you're much less probably to experience the hyperventilating that can make other signs and symptoms — and the panic attack itself — worse.

Consciousness on taking deep breaths inside and out through your mouth, feeling the air slowly fill your chest and stomach, after which slowly go away them once more. Breathe in for a count number of 4, hold for a second, and then breathe out for a be counted of 4:

2. Understand that you have a panic attack

Via spot which you have a panic attack in place of a coronary heart assault, you could remind yourself that this is transient, it'll skip, and that you're adequate.

Put off the worry that you'll be loss of life or that approaching doom is looming, each symptom of panic attacks. This may assist you to focus on other techniques to lessen your signs.

3. near your eyes

A few panic assaults come from triggers that weigh down you. In case you're in a quick-paced surroundings with plenty of stimuli, this will feed your panic attack.

To lessen the stimuli, close your eyes for the duration of your panic assault. This may block out any more stimuli and make it less complicated to cognizance of your breathing.

4. Exercise mindfulness

Mindfulness can assist floor you inside the fact of what's around you. Since panic attacks can cause a sense of detachment or separation from truth, this will fight your panic assault because it's drawing near or genuinely occurring.

Recognition at the physical sensations you're acquainted with, like digging your feet into the floor, or feeling the texture of your jeans to your hands. These unique sensations ground you firmly in fact and come up with something goal to awareness on.

5. Find a focus object

A few humans locate it useful to find a single object to consciousness, all in their interest during a panic attack. Pick out one object in clean sight and consciously word the whole thing approximately it viable.

6. Use muscle relaxation techniques

Just like deep breathing, muscle rest strategies can help prevent your panic assault in its tracks with the aid of controlling your frame's reaction as much as thinkable.

Consciously relax one muscle at a time, starting with something easy, just like the fingers to your hand, and pass your way up through your frame.

Muscle relaxation strategies can be best whilst you've practiced them ahead.

7. Photograph your satisfied area

Imagine yourself there, and try to focus on the information as a lot as feasible. Believe digging your toes into the warm sand, or smelling the pointy scent of pine timber.

This area should be quiet, calm, and enjoyable — no streets of New York or Hong Kong, no matter how a whole lot you love the cities in real lifestyles.

8. Have interaction in light workout

Endorphins hold the blood pumping in precisely the right away. It may help flood our body with endorphins that could enhance our temper. Due to the fact you're careworn, pick light exercising that's mild at the body, like strolling or swimming.

The exception to that is if you're hyperventilating or suffering from breathing. Do what you could to catch your breath first.

9. Maintain lavender handy

Lavender is thought of being soothing and strain-relieving. It may assist your frame relax. In case you realize you're susceptible to panic attacks, hold a few lavender essential oil accessible and positioned a few for your forearms while you experience a panic attack. Breathe inside the heady scent.

You may additionally strive for ingesting lavender or chamomile tea. Each is relaxing and soothing.

Lavender ought to not be combined with benzodiazepines. This combination can purpose severe drowsiness.

10. Repeat a mantra internally

Repeating a mantra internally may be enjoyable and reassuring, and it is able to provide you with something to grasp onto at some point of a panic attack.

Whether or not it's simply "This too shall bypass," or a mantra that speaks to you individually, repeat it on loop on your head until you experience the panic attack begin to subside.

11. Take benzodiazepines

Benzodiazepines may additionally help treat panic attacks if you take one as quickly as you feel an attack approaching.

Even as other approaches to the remedy of panic can be preferential, the sector of psychiatry has mentioned that there's a handful of folks who will neither reply completely (or in any respect in a few cases) to the other procedures listed in above and as such, could be dependent on pharmacological approaches to therapy.

These techniques often will encompass benzodiazepines, a number of which carry FDA approval for the remedy of this situation, including alprazolam (Xanax).

Because benzodiazepines are a prescription medicinal drug, you'll probably need a panic sickness analysis for you to have the medication accessible.

This medicine may be exceedingly addictive, and the frame can alter to it over the years. It must simplest be used sparingly and in instances of extreme want.

8. Interact in light workout

Endorphins hold the blood pumping in exactly the proper away. It could help flood our body with endorphins, which could enhance our mood. Due to the fact you're stressed, choose the mild workout that's mild on the body, like on foot or swimming.

The exception to that is in case you're hyperventilating or suffering from breathing. Do what you may to catch your breath first.

9. Keep violet on hand

Lavender is known for being soothing and stress-relieving. It could help your body loosen up. In case you recognize you're at risk of panic attacks, maintain a few lavender vital oil accessible and put some to your forearms when you enjoy a panic assault. Breathe inside the fragrance.

You may also try consuming lavender or chamomile tea. Each is relaxing and soothing.

Lavender must not be combined with benzodiazepines. This combination can motive excessive drowsiness.

10. Repeat a mantra internally

Repeating a mantra internally can be relaxing and reassuring, and it can come up with something to comprehend onto all through a panic assault.

Whether it's sincerely "This too shall bypass," or a mantra that speaks to you for my part, repeat it on loop to your head till you experience the panic assault start to subside.

11. Take benzodiazepines

Benzodiazepines may help treat panic assaults in case you take one as soon as you feel an assault approaching.

Even as different strategies to the remedy of panic can be preferential, the field of psychiatry has recounted that there's a handful of folks who will neither reply fully (or at all in a few cases) to the alternative strategies indexed in above and as such, may be dependent on pharmacological methods to remedy.

Those processes often will encompass benzodiazepines, some of which bring FDA approval for the treatment of this situation, consisting of alprazolam (Xanax).

Because benzodiazepines are a prescription medicinal drug, you'll probably want a panic sickness diagnosis that allows you to have the medicine on hand.

This medicinal drug may be pretty addictive, and the body can alter it through the years. It has to handiest been used sparingly and in instances of severe want.

Chapter 3

Anxiety Disorders and Anxiety Attacks

Do you warfare with anxiety? Right here's how to recognize the signs and symptoms, signs and symptoms, and extraordinary kinds of anxiety—and locate the relief you want.

What is an anxiety disease?

Anxiety is an ordinary response to danger, the body's automated combat-or-flight response that is brought on while you sense threatened, below strain, or are going through a hard scenario, together with a task interview, exam, or first date. Sparsely, anxiety isn't necessarily an awful element. It will let you to live alert and focused, spur you to motion, and encourage you to clear up issues. But when tension is constant or overwhelming—while worries and fears intrude along with your relationships and each day existence—you've probably crossed the line from everyday tension into the territory of an anxiety disorder.

Because anxiety disorders are a set of related conditions as opposed to a single ailment, symptoms can also range from character to individual. One character may additionally suffer from extreme tension assaults that strike without caution, even as some other receives panicky on the concept of mingling at a party. A person else may also battle with a disabling worry of riding, or uncontrollable, intrusive mind. But another may additionally stay in a constant country of anxiety, demanding about anything and the entirety. But no matter their distinct bureaucracy, all tension issues illicit an excessive worry or worry out of percentage to the situation at hand.

Whilst having an anxiety disease can be disabling, stopping you from living the life you need, it's important to understand which you're not on my own. Anxiety issues are a few of the maximum common mental health troubles—and are particularly treatable. After you understand your tension disorder, there are steps you can take to lessen the signs and symptoms and regain control of your lifestyles.

Do I have an anxiety disorder?

In case you identify with any of the subsequent seven signs and symptoms, and that they simply gained go away, you may be stricken by an anxiety disorder:

Are you constantly nerve-racking, concerned, or on edge?

Does your tension intrude together with your paintings, school, or own family obligations?

Are you plagued by way of fears which you recognize are irrational, however, can't shake?

Do you agree that something bad will manifest if certain things aren't executed in a positive manner?

Do you keep away from everyday conditions or activities due to the fact they cause you anxiety?

Do you revel in unexpected, sudden assaults of heart-pounding panic?

Do you experience like danger and disaster are around each corner?

Symptoms and symptoms of anxiety disorders

Similarly to the primary symptom of excessive and irrational fear and fear, other not unusual emotional signs of a tension disease include:

Feelings of apprehension or dread

Watching for signs and symptoms of danger

Looking forward to the worst

Hassle concentrating

Feeling nerve-racking and jumpy

Irritability

Feeling like your mind's gone clean

But tension is more than just a feeling. As fabricated from the frame's combat-or-flight response, anxiety also entails a huge variety of bodily signs, inclusive of:

Pounding heart

Sweating

Headaches

Stomach upset

Dizziness

Common urination or diarrhea

Shortness of breath

Muscle tension or twitches

Shaking or trembling

Insomnia

Due to those physical symptoms, tension sufferers regularly mistake their disease for scientific contamination. They may visit many medical doctors and make numerous journeys to the medical institution before their tension ailment is subsequently recognized.

What is a tension attack?

Tension attacks, also referred to as panic attacks, are episodes of intense panic or fear. Anxiety assaults typically occur all at once and without caution. From time to time, there's an obvious trigger—getting stuck in an elevator, for example, or thinking about the big speech you have to provide—but in different instances, the attacks come out of the blue.

Anxiety attacks generally top inside 10 mins, and that they are not often remaining extra than 30 minutes. But all through that quick time, you can revel in terror so severe that you feel as in case you're about to die or totally lose manipulate. The physical signs and symptoms of tension attacks are themselves so scary that many human beings think they have a coronary heart attack. After a tension attack is over, you can fear approximately having every other one, especially in a public place where help isn't to be had, or you couldn't without difficulty getaway.

Signs of a tension attack include:

Surge of overwhelming panic

Feeling of losing control or going crazy

Coronary heart palpitations or chest pain

Feeling such as you're going to pass out

Problem respiratory or choking sensation

Hyperventilation

Warm flashes or chills

Trembling or shaking

Nausea or stomach cramps

Feeling indifferent or unreal

It's essential to are seeking to assist if you're beginning to keep away from sure conditions due to the fact you're afraid of having a panic attack. The truth is that panic assaults are tremendously treatable. In fact, many humans are panic loose inside just five to 8 remedy classes.

Forms of anxiety disorders and their symptoms

Girl with phone ruminating tension issues and conditions intently related to anxiety problems encompass:

Generalized anxiety ailment (GAD)

If steady worries and fears distract you from your everyday activities, otherwise you're through a persistent feeling that something terrible is going to show up, you may be laid low with generalized anxiety sickness (GAD). Human beings with GAD are continual worrywarts who feel demanding nearly all the time, even though they may no longer even recognize why. Anxiety associated with GAD frequently manifests in bodily signs and symptoms like insomnia, belly dissatisfaction, restlessness, and fatigue.

Panic attacks and panic disease

Panic sickness is characterized with the aid of repeated, surprising panic assaults, in addition to worry of experiencing any other episode. Agoraphobia, the fear of being someplace where getaway or help might be hard on the occasion of a panic attack, might also accompany a panic disease. If you have agoraphobia, you're in all likelihood to keep away from public locations, which include shopping shops or confined spaces, including an airplane.

Obsessive-compulsive disease (OCD)

Obsessive-compulsive disease (OCD) is characterized by undesirable minds or behaviors that appear not possible to forestall or manage. If you have OCD, you may feel by means of obsessions, such as a routine fear which you forgot to turn off the oven or that you would possibly harm someone. You may also suffer from uncontrollable compulsions, together with washing your fingers again and again.

Phobias and irrational fears

A phobia is an unrealistic or exaggerated worry of a selected item, activity, or scenario that, during fact, gives little to no hazard. Commonplace phobias encompass fear of animals (along with snakes and spiders), fear of flying, and worry of heights. Inside the case of an extreme phobia, you may visit intense lengths to avoid the object of your worry. Regrettably, avoidance handiest strengthens the phobia.

Social anxiety ailment

If you have a debilitating fear of being viewed negatively via others and humiliated in public, you can have social anxiety disease, additionally known as social phobia. Social anxiety ailment can be a concept of as excessive shyness. In excessive instances, social situations are prevented altogether. Performance tension (better-called degree fright) is the most commonplace type of social phobia.

Publish-demanding strain disease (PTSD)

Post-stressful pressure disease (PTSD) is a severe anxiety ailment that could occur inside the aftermath of a stressful or existence-threatening occasion. PTSD can be the concept of a panic attack that rarely, if ever, we could up. Signs and symptoms of PTSD consist of flashbacks or nightmares about the incident, hypervigilance, startling effortlessly, withdrawing from others, and keeping off conditions that remind you of the event.

Separation tension sickness

Even as separation anxiety is an everyday degree of development, if anxieties intensify or are persistent sufficient to get inside the way of college or different sports, your baby may additionally have separation tension disorder. Children with separation anxiety ailment can also become agitated at just the concept of being far from mother or dad and bitch of sickness to avoid playing with buddies or going to high school.

Self-help for tension

A woman connecting smiling now, not all people who worry plenty, has a tension ailment. You could sense irritating due to a very demanding agenda, lack of workout or sleep, pressure at domestic or paintings, or maybe from too much caffeine. The bottom line is that if your lifestyle is bad and demanding, you're much more likely to sense demanding—whether or not or not, you truly have an anxiety disorder. These guidelines can help to decrease anxiety and control signs and symptoms of a sickness:

Connect with others. Loneliness and isolation can trigger or get worse tension, while speaking about your worries face to face can frequently cause them to seem much less overwhelming. Make it a point to regularly meet up with friends, be a part of a self-help or assist institution, or share your issues and issues with a depended on cherished one. If you don't have all and sundry you may reach out to, it's never too late to construct new friendships and a supportive community.

Control stress. If your stress ranges are through the roof, pressure control can assist. Have a look at your duties and notice if there are any you could surrender, turn down, or delegate to others.

Exercise relaxation techniques. When often practiced relaxation strategies, including mindfulness meditation, modern muscle rest, and deep respiration, can reduce tension signs and symptoms and growth feelings of relaxation and emotional nicely-being.

Workout is a herbal stress buster and anxiety reliever. To attain the most advantage, aim for at the least half-hour of aerobic exercise on most days (damaged up into short periods if that's simpler). Rhythmic sports that require transferring each of your arms and legs are especially effective. Strive strolling, strolling, swimming, martial arts, or dancing.

Be smart, approximately caffeine, alcohol, and nicotine. If you struggle with tension, you could want to recall reducing your caffeine intake or cutting it out completely. In addition, alcohol can also make anxiety worse. And at the same time, as it could seem like cigarettes are calming, nicotine is, in reality, a powerful stimulant that leads to higher, no longer lower, ranges of hysteria. To assist kicking the dependency, see the way to Stop Smoking.

Stressful is an intellectual habit; you can learn how to interrupt. Techniques together with creating a fear length, tough irritating mind, and studying just to accept uncertainty can significantly lessen worry and calm your annoying mind.

When to seek expert help for anxiety symptoms
Even as self-assist coping strategies for anxiety may be very powerful, in case your concerns, fears, or tension attacks have ended up so exquisite that they're causing extreme misery or disrupting your every day habitual, it's essential to seek professional help.

In case you're experiencing a number of physical tension signs, you should start through getting a clinical checkup. Your physician can test to ensure that your tension isn't because of a clinical condition, which includes a thyroid problem, hypoglycemia, or asthma. Considering that certain tablets and supplements can motive anxiety, your physician will also want to understand about any prescriptions, over the counter medications, natural remedies, and recreational pills you're taking.

If your health practitioner guidelines out a scientific cause, the next step is to talk over with a therapist who has reveled in treating tension issues. The therapist will work with you to determine the cause and kind of your tension sickness and devise a route of treatment.

Remedy for tension problems

Tension problems reply very well to remedy—and often in a distinctly quick amount of time. The precise treatment method depends on the type of tension disease and its severity. However, in standard, most tension disorders are treated with remedy, medication, or a few aggregate of the two. Cognitive-behavioral remedy and publicity remedy are sorts of behavioral remedy, that means they recognition on conduct as opposed to underlying mental conflicts or issues from the beyond. They can assist with troubles together with panic assaults, generalized anxiety, and phobias.

Cognitive-behavior therapy allows you to pick out and challenge the bad wondering patterns and irrational beliefs that fuel your tension.

Publicity remedy encourages you to confront your fears and anxieties in a safe, controlled environment. Thru gradual exposure to the scary object or scenario, either to your imagination or in truth, you advantage an extra sense of control. As you face your worry without being harmed, your tension will decrease.

Medicine for tension disorders

When you have tension that's severe enough to intrude with your capacity to feature, medication may additionally help relieve a few anxiety symptoms. But, anxiety medicinal drugs can be habit-forming and cause unwanted or maybe risky aspect results, so make sure to research your alternatives carefully. Many people use anti-anxiety remedy whilst remedy, exercise, or self-help strategies would include paintings simply as properly or higher—minus the facet effects and protection concerns. It's essential to weigh the benefits and dangers of tension medicine so that you could make a knowledgeable selection.

Approaches to certainly lessen tension

A few anxiety is an everyday a part of existence. It's a byproduct of residing in a frequently-chaotic international. Anxiety isn't all terrible, though. It makes you aware of danger, motivates you to stay organized and prepared, and facilitates you calculate dangers. Nonetheless, whilst anxiety will become an everyday war, it's time to act before it snowballs. Unchecked tension might also greatly affect you are nice of life. Take manipulate by trying out the ideas underneath.

1. Live active

Everyday exercising is good for your physical and emotional fitness. Ordinary exercising works as well as medicinal drugs to ease anxiety for a few human beings. And it's no longer only a quick-term restoration; you can experience tension alleviation for hours after working out.

2. Don't drink alcohol

Alcohol is a herbal sedative. Consuming a tumbler of wine or a finger of whiskey whilst your nerves are shot may calm you at first. Once the excitement is over, however, tension may additionally go back with a vengeance. In case you rely upon alcohol to relieve tension in place of treating the basis of the hassle, you can expand alcohol dependence.

3. Prevent smoking

People who smoke regularly attain a cigarette throughout disturbing times. Yet, like drinking alcohol, taking a drag on a cigarette whilst you're confused a brief restore that could get worse tension over the years. ResearchTrusted supply has shown that the earlier you start smoking in lifestyles, the better your risk of developing an anxiety sickness later. Research also shows nicotine, and different chemical substances in cigarette smoke modify pathways inside the mind linked to anxiety.

4. Ditch caffeine

When you have chronic tension, caffeine isn't always your buddy. Caffeine may also cause nervousness and jitters, neither of which is ideal if you're anxious. Studies have shown caffeine might also cause or worsen anxiety disorders. It is able to also reason panic attacks in humans with panic disease. In some humans, disposing of caffeine may additionally substantially enhance anxiety symptoms.

5. Get a few sleeps

Insomnia is a commonplace symptom of tension. Make sleep a concern via:

Handiest snoozing at night time when you're tired

No longer analyzing or watching tv in bed

Now not using your telephone, tablet, or pc in bed

No longer tossing and turning in your bed if you couldn't sleep; get up and go to every other room until you sense sleepy

Fending off caffeine, huge food, and nicotine earlier than bedtime

Preserving your room dark and cool

Writing down your worries earlier than going to bed

Going to sleep at the identical time each night

6. Meditate

The first-rate intention of meditation is to remove the chaotic mind out of your mind and update them with an experience of calm and mindfulness of the present second. Meditation is known for relieving strain and tension. Research from John Hopkins suggests 30 minutes of day by day meditation may additionally alleviate a few tension signs and symptoms and act as an antidepressant.

7. Eat a healthful diet

Low blood sugar tiers, dehydration, or chemicals in processed ingredients inclusive of artificial flavorings, artificial colorations, and preservatives may additionally cause mood changes in some human beings. A high-sugar weight-reduction plan may affect temperament. If your anxiety worsens after ingesting, take a look at your ingesting behavior. Live hydrated, eliminate processed foods, and eat a healthful food regimen rich in complex carbohydrates, end result and greens, and lean proteins.

8. Practice deep breathing

Shallow, speedy respiration is commonplace with anxiety. It could cause a quick coronary heart fee, dizziness or lightheadedness, or maybe a panic attack. Deep respiration sporting activities — the deliberate manner of taking sluggish, even, deep breaths — can help repair ordinary breathing patterns and decrease anxiety.

9. Attempt aromatherapy

Aromatherapy uses crucial aromatic oils to promote health and well-being. The oils can be inhaled at once or delivered to a heat bath or diffuser. Studies have proven that aromatherapy:

Allows you to relax

Allows you to sleep

Boosts mood

Reduces coronary heart charge and blood stress

Some essential oils used to alleviate tension are:

Bergamot

Lavender

Clary sage

Grapefruit

Ylang ylang

Keep online for bergamot, lavender, clary sage, grapefruit, and ylang-ylang vital oils.

10. Drink chamomile tea

A cup of chamomile tea is a commonplace home cure to calm frayed nerves and sell sleep. A 2009 study Trusted source confirmed chamomile could also be an effective best friend towards generalized anxiety ailment. The examination determined people who took German chamomile drugs (220 milligrams up to 5 instances each day) had a greater reduction in scores for checks that measure tension signs than people who had been given a placebo.

Right here's a variety of chamomile tea to strive.

Takeaway

If you're feeling irritating, attempting the above ideas may additionally assist calm you down. Recall, home remedies may additionally assist ease anxiety, but they don't update expert assist. Improved tension might also require remedy or prescription medicine. Talk to your health practitioner approximately your issues.

Simple ways to relieve pressure and anxiety

Strain and tension are common experiences for most of the people.

In fact, 70% of adults inside the US say they experience pressure or tension day by day.

Here are 16 easy ways to alleviate strain and tension.

1. Exercise

Workout is one of the most crucial things you may do to combat strain.

It'd appear contradictory; however, placing bodily pressure to your body via exercise can relieve intellectual stress.

The advantages are most powerful whilst you work out frequently. Those who exercise frequently are less probable to experience anxiety than those who don't work out.

There are some motives in the back of this:

Stress hormones: exercising lowers your frame's pressure hormones — inclusive of cortisol — ultimately. It also helps launch endorphins, which are chemical compounds that improve your mood and act as natural painkillers.

Sleep: workout can also improve your sleep great, which may be negatively affected by pressure and tension.

Self-belief: while you exercise often, you can sense extra equipped and confident on your body, which in flip promotes intellectual well-being.

Try and find a workout ordinary or interest you experience, which includes on foot, dancing, mountain climbing, or yoga.

Sports — which include on foot or going for walks — that involve repetitive moves of big muscle agencies may be especially stressing relieving.

Precis

Normal exercise can help decrease strain and tension with the aid of releasing endorphins and improving your sleep and self-picture.

2. Take into account dietary supplements

Numerous dietary supplements promote stress and tension reduction. Here is a short review of a number of the most not unusual ones:

A few supplements can interact with medicines or have aspect results so that you can also need to seek advice from a physician when you have a scientific circumstance.

Precis

Sure dietary supplements can reduce strain and anxiety, which include ashwagandha, omega-3 fatty acids, green tea, and lemon balm.

3. Mild a Candle

The usage of important oils or burning a scented candle may additionally help reduce your feelings of stress and tension.

Some scents are, in particular, soothing. Right here are some of the maximum calming scents:

Lavender

Rose

Vetiver

Bergamot

Roman chamomile

Neroli

Frankincense

Sandalwood

Ylang ylang

Orange or orange blossom

Geranium

Using scents to deal with your mood is known as aromatherapy. Numerous research shows that aromatherapy can lower anxiety and improve sleep (7Trusted supply, 8Trusted source, 9Trusted supply).

Precis

Aromatherapy can assist decrease tension and stress. Light a candle or use crucial oils to gain from calming scents.

Four. Reduce Your Caffeine intake

Caffeine is a stimulant determined in espresso, tea, chocolate, and power liquids. High doses can reduce growth tension (10Trusted source).

Humans have one of a kind thresholds for away a good deal of caffeine they can tolerate.

If you word that caffeine makes you jittery or anxious, don't forget slicing lower back.

Although many studies show that coffee can be wholesome in moderation, it is no longer for anyone. In well-known, five or fewer cups in keeping with day is taken into consideration a moderate quantity.

Summary

Excessive quantities of caffeine can cause growth strain and anxiety. However, human beings' sensitivity to caffeine can range substantially.

5. Write It Down

One way to deal with strain is to jot down matters down.

At the same time as recording what you are stressed about is one technique, some other is jotting down what you are grateful for.

Gratitude may additionally assist relieve strain and anxiety by focusing your mind on what is nice for your lifestyles.

Precis

Keeping a journal can assist relieve pressure and tension, in particular if you recognition at the advantageous.

6. Bite Gum

For an extraordinary easy and short stress reliever, strive chewing a stick of gum.

One study confirmed that those who chewed gum had an extra feel of wellbeing and decrease strain.

One feasible explanation is that chewing gum reasons brain waves just like the ones at ease humans. Another is that chewing gum promotes blood go with the flow on your mind.

Additionally, one latest have a look at found that strain comfort became greatest while humans chewed greater strongly.

Keep for chewing gum on-line.

Summary

In line with several research, chewing gum may additionally assist you loosen up. It is able to promote wellbeing and reduce pressure additionally.

7. Spend Time With pals and family

Social guides from pals and family will let you get through disturbing instances.

Being a part of a friend network offers you a sense of belonging and self-confidence, which assist you in hard instances.

One takes a look at discovered that for ladies mainly, spending time with buddies and youngsters helps launch oxytocin, a herbal stress reliever. This impact is called "tend and befriend," and is the other of the fight-or-flight reaction (13Trusted supply).

Keep in mind that each men and women gain from friendship.

Some other studies observed that men and women with the fewest social connections have been more likely to suffer from despair and tension (14Trusted supply).

Precis

Having robust social ties might also assist you get thru demanding instances and lower your risk of tension.

8. Chortle

It's hard to sense stressful while you're giggling. It's proper to your health, and there are a few ways it may help relieve stress:

A look at among people with cancer determined that human beings within the laughter intervention group skilled more strain remedy than those who have been sincerely distracted.

Strive to look a humorous television display or striking out with buddies who make you laugh.

Precis

Discover the humor in regular life, spend time with funny friends, or watch a comedy show to assist relieve strain.

9. Study to say No

Not all stressors are inside your manipulate, but some are.

Take manage over the parts of your lifestyles that you can change and are inflicting your stress.

One way to do this could be to mention "no" greater regularly.

This is mainly real if you find yourself taking up extra than you can manage, as juggling many obligations can depart you feeling beaten.

Being selective about what you are taking on — and pronouncing no to things in an effort to unnecessarily uploading on your load — can lessen your stress ranges.

Precis

Try no longer to take on greater than you can deal with. Saying no is one way to control your stressors.

10. Learn how to avoid Procrastination

Every other manner of taking manage of your pressure is to live on pinnacle of your priorities and prevent procrastinating.

Procrastination can lead you to behave reactively, leaving you scrambling to capture up. This may cause pressure, which negatively affects your fitness and sleep quality (sixteen).

Get within the addiction of creating a to-do listing prepared by means of priority. Give yourself realistic deadlines and paintings your manner down the list.

Paintings on the matters that want to get performed today and deliver your self-chunks of uninterrupted time, as switching between duties or multitasking can be demanding it.

Precis

Prioritize what needs to get finished and make time for it. Staying on top of your to-do listing can help ward off procrastination-associated pressure.

11. Take a Yoga class

Yoga has come to be a popular method of strain alleviation and workout among all age organizations.

Even as yoga styles differ, most proportion a common aim — to enroll in your frame and thoughts.

Yoga usually does this by way of growing frame and breath attention.

Some research has examined yoga's impact on mental fitness. Normal studies have observed that yoga can decorate temper and might also be as effective as antidepressant tablets at treating despair and tension.

But, a lot of that research is confined, and there are nevertheless questions on how yoga works to reap strain discount.

In standard, the advantage of yoga for strain and tension seems to be associated with its impact on your anxious machine and stress response.

It could help decrease cortisol tiers, blood stress and heart fee, and boom gamma-aminobutyric acid (GABA), a neurotransmitter. This is diminished in temper disorders.

Summary

Yoga is broadly used for strain discount. It can assist lower pressure hormone tiers and blood pressure.

12. Exercise Mindfulness

Mindfulness describes practices that anchor you to the prevailing second.

It may assist combat the anxiety-inducing consequences of bad questioning.

There are numerous methods for growing mindfulness, consisting of mindfulness-primarily based cognitive remedy, mindfulness-based stress discount, yoga, and meditation.

The latest look at university students advised that mindfulness may also help boom vanity, which in turn lessens signs and symptoms of anxiety and despair.

13. Cuddle

Cuddling, kissing, hugging, and sex can all assist relieve stress (19Trusted supply, 20Trusted supply).

Superb bodily touch can help launch oxytocin and decrease cortisol. This will help decrease blood stress and heart rate, each of which can be physical signs of strain.

Apparently, human beings aren't the only animals who cuddle for pressure alleviation. Chimpanzees additionally cuddle friends who're burdened.

Precis

Fantastic touch from cuddling, hugging, kissing, and sex can also assist lower stress by using liberating oxytocin and reducing blood stress.

14. Listen to Soothing song

Taking note of music will have a completely enjoyable impact on the body.

Gradual-paced instrumental song can result in the relaxation response by means of assisting decrease blood pressure and coronary heart charge in addition to strain hormones.

Some kinds of classical, Celtic, local American and Indian music can be especially soothing, but honestly paying attention to the music you revel in is powerful too.

Nature sounds can also be very calming. That is why they're frequently included in rest and meditation song.

Summary

Listening to tune you like can be a good manner to alleviate pressure.

15. Deep breathing

Intellectual stress turns on your sympathetic anxious machine, signaling your frame to enter the "combat-or-flight" mode.

Deep respiration exercises can assist prompt your parasympathetic worried gadget, which controls the rest response.

There are several types of deep respiratory physical activities, together with diaphragmatic breathing, stomach respiration, stomach breathing, and paced breathing.

The intention of deep breathing is to cognizance your awareness for your breath, making it slower and deeper. When you breathe in deeply through your nostrils, your lungs fully make bigger, and your stomach rises.

This facilitates sluggish your coronary heart fee, permitting you to experience greater nonviolent.

This video explains how to exercise diaphragmatic respiration.

Summary

Deep breathing activates the relaxation reaction. More than one strategies allow you to learn how to breathe deeply.

16. Spend Time along with your puppy

Having a pet may assist reduce stress and enhance your mood.

Interacting with pets may also assist release oxytocin, a brain chemical that promotes an advantageous mood (23Trusted source).

Having a puppy can also help relieve strain with the aid of supplying you with reason, retaining your energetic and imparting companionship — all traits that help reduce anxiety.

Summary

Spending time with your pet is a peaceful, exciting way to lessen strain.

Rest strategies That Zap stress rapid

Relax. You deserve it, it is excellent for you, and it takes much less time than you believe you studied.

1. Meditate

A couple of minutes of exercise, according to today, can help ease anxiety. "studies suggests that everyday meditation might also regulate the mind's neural pathways, making you more resilient to strain," says psychologist Robbie Maller Hartman, Ph.D., a Chicago fitness and wellness coach.

It is easy. Sit up with each foot at the ground. Near your eyes. Cognizance your attention on reciting -- out loud or silently -- a fantastic mantra together with "I sense at peace" or "I like myself." region one hand on your stomach to sync the chant along with your breaths. Allow any distracting mind drift by like clouds.

2. Breathe Deeply

Take a five-minute spoil and cognizance on your respiratory. Sit up straight, eyes shut, with a hand in your stomach. Slowly gasp through your nose, feeling the breath start on your abdomen and work its manner to the top of your head.

You may LIKE

"Deep respiratory counters the consequences of strain via slowing the coronary heart price and lowering blood pressure," psychologist Judith Tutin, PhD, says. She's an authorized lifestyle train in Rome, GA.

3. Be present

"Take five minutes and awareness on best one conduct with consciousness," Tutin says. Observe how the air feels in your face when you're taking walks and the way your feet feel hitting the floor. Enjoy the texture and flavor of each chunk of meals.

When you spend time within the moment and consciousness of your senses, you must feel much less irritating.

4. Attain Out

Your social community is one in every of your great equipment for coping with stress. Talk to others -- ideally face to face, or at least at the cellphone — proportion of what is occurring. You can get a clean angle at the same time as retaining your connection sturdy.

5. Track In in your frame

Mentally scan your frame to get a sense of how pressure affects it every day. Lie for your back, or sit down along with your feet at the floor. Begin at your ft and paintings your manner up on your scalp, noticing how your frame feels.

"truly be aware of locations you experience tight or unfastened without trying to exchange something," Tutin says. For 1 to two mins, consider each deep breath flowing to that body element. Repeat this system as you pass your cognizance up your frame, paying close attention to sensations you feel in every frame part.

6. Decompress

Vicinity a warm warmth wrap around your neck and shoulders for 10 mins. Near your eyes and relax your face, neck, upper chest, and back muscle groups. Take away the wrap, and use a tennis ball or foam curler to rub down away anxiety.

7. Laugh Out Loud

A very good stomach snort doesn't just lighten the load mentally. It lowers cortisol, your frame's stress hormone, and boosts brain chemicals referred to as endorphins, which assist your mood. Lighten up by way of tuning in to your preferred sitcom or video, reading the comics, or speaking to a person who makes you smile.

8. Crank Up the Tunes

Research shows that listening to soothing song can lower blood strain, heart fee, and anxiety. Permit your thoughts to consciousness at the unique melodies, devices, or singers within the piece," Benninger says. You can also blow off steam by using rocking out to greater upbeat tunes -- or singing at the pinnacle of your lungs!

9. Get transferring

You don't have to run that allows you to get a runner's excessive. All styles of exercise, which includes yoga and strolling, can ease melancholy and tension by supporting the mind release sense-desirable chemical substances and by means of giving your frame a danger to exercise coping with strain. You can go for a quick stroll around the block, take the stairs up and down a few flights, or do some stretching exercises like head rolls and shoulder shrugs.

10. be thankful

Maintain a gratitude magazine or several (one via your mattress, one for your handbag, and one at work) to help you don't forget all of the things which might be right for your lifestyles.

Use these journals to appreciate excellent studies like an infant's smile, a sunshine-crammed day, and accurate health. Don't neglect to celebrate accomplishments like learning a brand new undertaking at paintings or a new hobby.

While you start feeling stressed, spend a couple of minutes looking through your notes to remind yourself what actually subjects.

Chapter 4

Anxiety: Stop Negative Thoughts

Tension is having too much fear and worry. A few human beings have what's known as generalized tension disorder. They feel concerned and harassed about many stuff. Regularly they worry about even small things. A few human beings additionally might also have panic attacks. A panic assault is a sudden feeling of intense anxiety.

Human beings who've social tension disorder worry that they will do or say the wrong component and embarrass themselves around others.

Anxiety can motive physical symptoms like a fast heartbeat and sweaty palms. It could make you limit your activities and can make it difficult to revel in your existence.

Healthful thinking can help you save you or manipulate tension.

A bad mind can increase your worry or worry.

Cognitive-behavioral remedy, or CBT, is a kind of remedy that can help you update bad mind with correct, encouraging ones.

Converting your thinking will make an effort. You want to practice healthy questioning each day. After a while, healthy thinking will come obviously to you.

Wholesome thinking may not be sufficient to help some human beings who've fear and anxiety. Name your health practitioner or therapist in case you assume you need greater assist.

How can you operate wholesome questioning to cope with anxiety?

Word and stop your mind

Step one is to observe and stop your terrible thoughts or "self-speak." Self-talk is what you observed and accept as true with about yourself and your reports. It is like a walking observation to your head. Yourself-talk can be rational and beneficial. Or it could be bad and now not useful.

Ask about your thoughts

The next step is to ask yourself whether or not your mind is beneficial or unhelpful. Observe what you are announcing to yourself. Does the proof assist your terrible notion? Some of yourself-speak may be genuine. Or it may be partially proper, however, exaggerated.

One of the pleasant approaches to look in case you are stressful an excessive amount of is to examine the chances. What are the percentages, or chances, that the terrible element you're involved in approximately will occur? When you have a task review that has one small complaint among many compliments, what are the chances that you certainly are at risk of dropping your activity? The odds are probably low.

There are numerous kinds of irrational minds. Here are some sorts of searching for:

You filter out the best and consciousness best at the bad. Example: "I get so nervous talking in public. I realize that people are considering how bad I am at speak Me." fact: possibly no person is extra focused on your performance than you. It is able to help to search for a few evidence that proper matters befell after one of your shows. Did humans applaud in a while? Did all and sundry let you know which you did a very good process?

Need to: human beings every now and then have set ideas about how they "ought to" act. If you listen yourself announcing that you or different humans "ought to," "have to," or "ought to" do something, then you might be placing your self up to sense horrific. Instance: "I must be in control all of the time, or I cannot deal with matters." truth: there's not anything wrong with wanting to have some control over the things that you could control. However, you could purpose yourself tension by means of worrying about matters which you can't control.

Overgeneralizing: This is taking one example and announcing it is authentic for the whole lot. Look for words that include "in no way" and "continually." For example: "I will by no means experience regular. I worry about the entirety all the time." reality: you could worry approximately many things. However, the whole lot? Is it feasible for you're exaggerating? Although you may worry approximately many things, you furthermore may also locate that you feel robust and calm about different things.

All-or-not anything questioning: this is also called black-or-white questioning. Instance: "If I don't get an excellent process overview, then I'll lose my process." truth: most overall performance critiques consist of a few constructive grievances—something you can see paintings on to improve. If you get five nice remarks and one constructive proposal, that may be a right to evaluate. It doesn't mean that you're in the chance of losing your task.

Catastrophic thinking: this is assuming that the worst will appear. This kind of irrational thinking regularly consists of "what if" questions. Example: "I have been having complications currently. I'm so involved. What if it's a brain tumor?" fact: when you have masses of complications, you must see a health practitioner. But the odds are that it is something more commonplace and away less critical. You might need glasses. You could have a sinus contamination. Perhaps you're getting tension headaches from pressure.

Select your thoughts

The subsequent step is to select a helpful idea to update the unhelpful one.

Retaining a journal of your mind is one of the exceptional approaches to practice preventing, asking, and deciding on your mind. It makes you privy to your self-communicate. Write down any bad or unhelpful thoughts you had throughout the day. If you think you might not take into account them at the give up of your day, hold a notepad with you so that you can write down any mind as they occur. Then write down beneficial messages to correct the poor thoughts.

In case you try this each day, an accurate, beneficial mind will quickly come clearly to you.

However, there can be a few realities in some of your negative minds. You may have some stuff you want to work on. If you failed to carry out in addition to you would really like on something, write that down. You can create paintings on a plan to accurate or improve that area.

Tremendous questioning: prevent bad self-talk from lessening strain

Effective thinking facilitates pressure management and might even improve your health. Exercise overcoming bad self-speak with examples supplied.

Is your glass half-empty or half-complete? The way you solve this age-old query approximately nice questioning may reflect your outlook on existence, your mindset towards your self, and whether you're positive or pessimistic — and it may even have an effect on your health.

Certainly, some research displays that persona trends such as optimism and pessimism can have an effect on many areas of your health and properly-being. The high-quality wondering that normally comes with optimism is a key part of effective strain control. And effective pressure control is associated with many health blessings. In case you have a tendency to be pessimistic, don't despair — you could study fantastic questioning skills.

Understanding wonderful thinking and self-communicate

Superb thinking doesn't suggest that you maintain your head within the sand and ignore lifestyle's much less excellent situations. Tremendous wondering simply way which you approach unpleasantness in an extra fantastic and productive way. You suspect the fine goes to show up, not the worst.

Superb thinking frequently starts off evolved with self-talk. Self-communicate is the limitless movement of unspoken mind that run through your head. This automatic mind can be tremendous or negative. Some of your self-talk comes from common sense and reason. Different self-communicate can also rise up from misconceptions which you create because of a lack of information.

If the mind that runs through your head is generally bad, your outlook on life is much more likely pessimistic. If your thoughts are, in most cases, advantageous, you're in all likelihood an optimist — someone who practices positive wondering.

The health benefits of superb questioning

Researchers hold to discover the consequences of high-quality thinking and optimism on fitness. Health advantages that fantastic thinking might also provide consist of:

Expanded existence span

Lower fees of depression

Lower levels of distress

More resistance to the common bloodless

Better mental and physical well-being

Better cardiovascular fitness and decreased danger of demise from cardiovascular ailment

Better coping abilities at some point of hardships and times of strain

It's doubtful why folks who interact in advantageous wondering enjoy these fitness advantages. One theory is that having a wonderful outlook enables you to cope higher with disturbing situations, which reduces the dangerous health consequences of stress in your body.

It's also thought that fine and optimistic humans have a tendency to stay more healthy lifestyles — they get more bodily interest, observe a healthier weight-reduction plan, and do not smoke or drink alcohol in excess.

Identifying bad questioning

Now not positive if your self-talk is fine or negative? A few not unusual sorts of terrible self-communicate consist of:

Filtering. You magnify the terrible components of a state of affairs and filter out all the effective ones. As an example, you had a superb day at paintings. You finished your responsibilities beforehand of time and had been complimented for doing a rapid and thorough task.

Personalizing. While something terrible occurs, you robotically blame yourself. For example, you listen that a night out with friends is canceled, and also you expect that the change in plans is because nobody wanted to be around you.

Catastrophizing. You routinely anticipate the worst. The force-thru espresso shop gets your order incorrect, and also you mechanically assume that the relaxation of your day may be a disaster.

Polarizing. You see matters best as either good or horrific. There may be no center floor. You sense that you have to be ideal, or you're a total failure.

That specializes in advantageous questioning

You can research to turn poor questioning into advantageous wondering. The method is straightforward. However, it does take time and exercise — you're creating a brand new dependency, in spite of everything. Here are some approaches to think and behave in a more advantageous and constructive manner:

Discover areas to trade. If you want to end up greater constructive and interact in more fantastic wondering, first perceive areas of your lifestyles which you usually suppose negatively approximately, whether it is paintings, your day by day shuttle or a relationship. You can begin small with the aid of focusing on one vicinity to technique in a more advantageous manner.

Check yourself. Periodically at some point of the day, stop and compare what you're wondering. In case you find that your mind is specifically terrible, try to find a way to put an effective spin on them.

Observe a healthy way of life. Aim to exercise for approximately 30 minutes on the maximum days of the week. You may also spoil it up into 10-minute chunks of time all through the day. Exercise can positively have an effect on temper and decrease stress. Comply with a wholesome food regimen to gasoline your thoughts and body. And study strategies to control pressure.

Surround yourself with advantageous human beings. Ensure those for your lifestyles are fantastic, supportive human beings you can rely upon to present useful advice and feedback. Terrible humans may additionally grow your stress stage and make you doubt your ability to manage strain in wholesome ways.

Practice effective self-speak. Begin by using the following one easy rule: don't say anything to yourself, which you would not say to anybody else. Be gentle and inspiring with yourself. If a terrible concept enters your mind, compare it rationally, and reply with affirmations of what is right about you. Think about things you're thankful for your existence.

Tension and bad mind

Worry is defined as having a habitual mind that create apprehension inside you and an expectation that sincerely something negative will occur within the destiny. Worry is worry approximately destiny. You may worry about what is going to manifest the following time you see that person you are interested in relationship. Or you may fear approximately whether or now not the shortness of breath you're experiencing is an indication of coronary heart sickness. For many years now, science has seen worry as a symptom of tension. But it sincerely takes place in despair as nicely.

Rumination is slightly different and is characterized as having a poor mind about something that occurred in the past. It generally entails thinking about how you had been not as exact at something as you would really like to be. In rumination, you may suppose over and over once more about how badly you performed in that remaining tennis suit; or how badly you sense about ignoring someone at the opera remaining night time. Rumination has been seen as greater of a symptom of melancholy; however, it also takes place in tension.

Fear and rumination are specific; however, they may be additionally similar in that they're each form of repetitive mind which might be unproductive. They each contain having intrusive, repetitive, extended, and uncontrollable mind approximately destiny or beyond reviews. Extra than that, they frequently occur collectively within an equal individual.

In other phrases, rumination and fear are symptoms of anxiety. And they're additionally a hassle that can be improved with remedy.

Examples of bad thoughts

There are numerous varieties of negative minds, and if you learn how to apprehend them, it will less complicate to decrease them and the impact they have got upon you. Right here are a few examples of poor thoughts:

Questioning that the person who wouldn't let you into the luxury branch store after hours was an awful individual due to the fact they didn't understand how vital you are.

Worrying, if you're out past due, that you will get in trouble with your partner in case you don't rush home and soon.

Worrying again and again approximately whether or not or no longer your boss will assume that the presentation you will make tomorrow is good.

You are worrying that the weakness to your leg is an indication which you are growing multiple sclerosis.

Traumatic that you may have nothing of interest to say to all people at the party you are going to this nighttime.

Repetitive bad mind Create poor feelings

Alternatively, if you sit down and purposefully think effective thoughts — perhaps you believe the day of your marriage to the man or woman you like and to be able to make you experience satisfied and properly inside.

So your thoughts do play a function in determining your mood, and clinical research has proven that there may be an affiliation among bad mind and anxiety and melancholy. In different phrases, people who have recurring cycles of terrible thoughts are more likely to be concerned or depressed. But, in case you think an advantageous mind, you'll be much more likely to be satisfied.

Your bad mind doesn't motivate you've got a terrible mood within the first area. However, what they do is this: after you are in a terrible temper — be it anxiety, depression, or each — your bad thoughts will maintain and deepen your terrible mood.

This is a good motive to find a manner to diminish the strength your terrible concept has over your life. You could both try and prevent having a bad mind, replace your poor thoughts with superb or, most of all, to forestall believing your negative thoughts.

Routine bad mind Create tales, and you then live in the memories of the ones

Routine cycles of negative mind create tales. They are much like the film's interior of your thoughts. Perhaps a circulation of thoughts will create a tale in which anybody thinks you're silly. Or maybe a move of thoughts will create a tale wherein criticize yourself for something you stated in your boss the alternative day.

Streams of negative mind also distort and tarnish the coolest intentions of your genuine self. Terrible thoughts create terrible stories, and you live in those memories as opposed to being your authentic self.

Think, for example, you spot a vacationer being abusive and advanced to someone who lives in the USA. He's journeying. He's ordering the individual neighborhood round and criticizing them. You have the impulse — out of goodness — to prevent this abuse. You walk over to the visitor, and in a kind and respectful manner, ask him to be type and gentle, and despite the fact that he's a chunk abashed, the whole thing works out simply first-class. The traveler realizes he's unkind and prevents.

However, think you're within the identical scenario, and a movement of negative thoughts is going for walks through your thoughts that depict the vacationer as a terrible character who's usual of the people who come from his United States of America, and also you get irritated. You march over to the vacationer, and inside the full flush of your righteous indignation, you are haughty and vital with him, and he becomes green with envy and defiant. Now he turns on you.

In that second, you had been residing in a tale created through your poor thoughts and the anger they generated, and by using acting out that story, you created every other trouble.

That is a second cause to find a way to diminish the energy of your bad thoughts.

There are right techniques for disempowering your poor thoughts

Routine negative mind is a hassle while you accept as true with they are actual. In case you are privy to your bad thoughts and don't accept as true with them, they may not motive any troubles. They will float by way of on your circulation of consciousness and dissolve.

The import of know-how that it is the act of believing your thoughts that makes them tricky and pathogenic is that the maximum of the therapeutic techniques for treating and disempowering poor thoughts are techniques that help pull you far away from believing those mind. Right here's an explanatory listing of those strategies:

Meditation changes your thoughts in several one-of-a-kind approaches. One of the first matters it does is create a scenario in that you stand out of doors of, and emerge as aware of, your movement of mind. In this case, there are entities found in your revel in your thoughts. There's your stream of mind, and there is the notice — that's you — that is looking at the stream of attention. It's far similar to the enjoyment of standing on a financial institution subsequent to a river and looking that river flow by means of.

Via status outside of your circulation of mind, you get rid of yourself from the midst of this mind, and this gives you the opportunity to forestall believing them. You may watch them cross through without believing them. This can both diminish and disempower your negative thoughts. Much less poor thoughts will get up, and after they do rise up, you'll have the choice of no longer believing them.

The first step on this technique is to discover ways to meditate on an item and allow your movement of mind passes by without repressing or maintaining onto any of them. Subsequently, you can learn to perceive the bad tales that your thoughts are telling you. And that sets you up to stop believing that they're proper. That is liberating.

Notion Journals thought journals work at an equal premise. They give you the possibility to get outside of your thoughts and get a more objective perspective on them. First, you become aware of the contents of your bad thoughts, and then you definitely write them down on your magazine. This makes you aware of your thoughts, receive you outdoor them, and let in you to assess them and decide whether or not or not they may be authentic.

Cognitive Behavioral remedy and Cognitive Restructuring can be done in cognitive behavioral remedy, or you can do it on your very own. But, it's far strongly endorsed which you do that method with a therapist.

Cognitive restructuring is a manner in that you discover your poor thought styles, after which they dispute them. In other words, cognitive restructuring is a technique in that you look at your poor mind and set up that they may be now not actual.

There are five levels to cognitive restructuring:

Discover and report - the primary element to do is to discover your poor mind and file them in a magazine. Also, report the state of affairs in that you had every bout of poor mental and the way the thoughts made you sense. This may begin the system of setting apart yourself out of your negative mind.

Examine - analyze the mind for your thought journal. Look for patterns within the subject matters of your mind. Do your thoughts create poor snapshots of yourself? What are the negative images they create? Appearance to see what varieties of situations trigger your negative mind. Maximum of all, analyze the thoughts to look if they're clearly proper.

Dispute - this is simply what it seems like. Critique your terrible thoughts if you assume they are not real. Mission them. In case you have a tendency to think you're a failure, remember to thoughts instances when you have been not a failure. In case you tend to suppose which you are usually a failure in social situations, recollect to mind events in which you and some other man or woman felt near each other. Yet again, this is approximately locating a manner to stop believing your poor thoughts.

Effective thoughts - when bad mind come up, replace them with superb thoughts. "I did experience myself at that ultimate birthday party I went to." "At final week's assembly, absolutely everyone notion my marketing strategy became super, and we used the plan with a few mild changes."

Practical dreams - negative thoughts are regularly the handmaiden of getting unrealistic photos of and goals for yourself. Both you want to be first-rate in the whole thing you do. Otherwise, you might be asking yourself to be a person you aren't. This form of self-photograph is a setup for poor thoughts. You will frequently be a failure in your personal eyes, and this may provide an upward thrust to a poor mind. Increase sensible desires to your paintings' life and your social life. This can lessen your bad self-photographs and bad thoughts.

A couple of things no longer to do

Do not choose your mind - a totally beneficial issue to do is to make sure now not to choose your poor thoughts. In case you judge them, you'll most effectively make extra of them come. Plus, you may feel terrible about yourself as a result of your judgments. Make friends along with your negative mind. Don't be fearful of them. Accept them without judging them, and learn rather to stop believing them.

Don't try to stop Your thoughts - Don't try and forestall your negative mind. This will handiest make greater of them come. Once more, the essence of what you need to be doing along with your terrible mind is to prevent believing them in a single manner or every other.

Recommendations to exchange poor thinking

Negative wondering contributes to tension in social and overall performance conditions. Maximum remedies for social tension contain an element committed to changing terrible wondering patterns into greater beneficial and positive ways of searching at situations.

The key to converting your terrible mind is to recognize how you believe you studied now (and the issues that result) and then use techniques to alternate mind or cause them to have less effect.

Typically, these steps are executed with a therapist; however, they also can be used as part of a self-help attempt towards overcoming social tension.

Understand your wondering styles

One of the first steps closer to changing your bad questioning styles understands exactly how you believe you studied properly now. Here's a list of 10 varieties of "faulty" wondering patterns that are probably getting you into trouble.

For example, in case you have a tendency to view yourself as an entire success or failure in every state of affairs, then you definitely are undertaking "black-and-white" questioning.

These ten thinking patterns range in subtle approaches; however, all of them contain distortions of truth and irrational ways of looking at conditions and those.

A way to stop wondering negatively

One of the basic elements of a treatment plan concerning cognitive-behavioral remedy (CBT) is cognitive restructuring. This manner lets you identify and change your terrible thoughts into greater useful and adaptive responses.

Whether or not accomplished in remedy or on your own, cognitive restructuring includes a step-through-step process whereby bad thoughts are recognized, evaluated for accuracy, and then replaced.

Although at the start, it is hard to suppose with this new style, over time and with exercise, positive and rational thoughts will come more naturally.

A way to deal with grievance

Similarly to cognitive restructuring, any other thing of CBT that is sometimes useful entails something known as the "assertive defense of the self." because it's far possible that a number of the time, humans will truly be essential and judgmental, it's miles important which you are capable of cope with rejection.

This technique is generally performed in therapy with a pretend conversation among you and your therapist to accumulate your assertiveness abilities and assertive responses to the grievance. Those competencies are then transferred to the actual global through homework assignments.

How to exercise Mindfulness

Mindfulness has its roots in meditation. It's far the practice of detaching yourself from your mind and feelings and viewing them as an outdoor observer.

All through mindfulness schooling, you may discover ways to view your thoughts and emotions as items floating past you that you could stop and observe or permit bypass you by using.

The goal of mindfulness is to advantage manipulate your emotional reactions to situations via permitting the wondering a part of your brain to take over.

Why thought stopping does not image

Notion stopping is the other of mindfulness. It's far the act of being in search of a negative mind and insisting that they're eliminated.

The hassle with concept preventing is that the greater you attempt to prevent your bad mind, the extra they'll floor. Mindfulness is finest to thought stopping as it offers much less weight to your thoughts and decreases the effect they have on you.

Notion preventing would possibly appear to help inside the short-term; however, within the lengthy-term, it ends in more anxiety.

Information idea Diaries

Concept diaries are tools that may be used as part of any manner to change terrible questioning. Concept diaries help you to become aware of your poor questioning styles and gain a better understanding of ways your thoughts (and now not the situations you're in) purpose your emotional reactions.

Most cognitive-behavioral remedy plans will contain the usage of a thought diary that you will complete as a part of daily homework assignments.

Sample idea Diary

Not sure what a real thought diary looks like? Here's a pattern shape that you may use to document your mind and examine the relationship between your terrible questioning styles and your emotional reactions.

How to finish a thought Diary

Here's a step-by means of-step description of how to fill out a thought diary just like the pattern from above.

On this specific example, we wreck down the concept manner of a person on a date, and the emotional and bodily reactions that result from terrible wondering patterns.

By using the end of the idea evaluation, we've replaced the irrational mind approximately rejection with more helpful and fantastic ways of thinking.

Can a bad mind Be Stopped?

The motive of your depression will be a physical illness, life activities, and personality problems, side effects from capsules, or mixtures of these factors. Your medical doctor's desire for treatment — or no treatment — could be based totally upon symptom frequency and test outcomes.

A flow of sad thoughts via your thoughts may be frustrating due to the fact you cannot be sure if depression is making you suspect negatively, or questioning negatively is making you depressed. A common bloodless, exhaustion, strain, starvation, sleep deprivation, even allergic reactions can make you depressed, which results in poor thoughts.

In many instances, depression may be resulting from negative questioning itself. Our emotions observe what we are thinking, and dwelling upon terrible thoughts can ship us spiraling down into depression. This idea is the guiding principle in the back of Cognitive behavior therapy (CBT) that evolved in the 1960s by Dr. Aaron T. Beck at the University of Pennsylvania.

To fight negative questioning, it is essential to recognize it. The subsequent are some cognitive distortions — ways that our mind convinces us of untruths. These distortions are typically used to boost bad questioning or emotions. By means of time and again refuting distortions, poor thinking will lessen.

A credit score is going to David D. Burns, writer of "Feeling appropriate: the new mood remedy" (HarperCollins, 1999), for coining commonplace names for those distortions.

Filtering: You stay absolutely upon a dust speck you note on a Van Gogh painting.

Polarized questioning: if you're not perfect, you are a failure. People are both tremendous and lousy.

Overgeneralization: You fell off the pony for your first try. Therefore you will fall each time you get on a saddle.

Personalization: everything that occurs is about you. Your exceptional buddy commenced gambling tennis due to the fact he is aware of you do not like the sport.

Control Fallacies: You sense like a helpless victim of outside forces. Or, you feel, in my view, answerable for each person's happiness.

Fallacy of equity: you are the simplest person who knows what's truthful, and you're sure that you are being handled unfairly.

Blaming: You blame others for your pain. Or, you blame yourself for the whole thing.

There are policies that ought to be obeyed via each person. In case you violate the rules, you sense responsibility. If others spoil the rules, you experience irritation.

Emotional Reasoning: My feelings outline the fact. I feel unpleasant. Consequently, I am unpleasant.

Fallacy of change: you observed you could change human beings to make your self-satisfied.

International Labeling: An intense shape of generalizing with exaggerated and emotionally loaded labels for yourself and others. You fail a quiz and make contact with yourself as a "lifetime loser."

Heaven's praise Fallacy: if you work difficult and sacrifice, you may usually be rewarded. If that reward would not come whilst you want it, you turn out to be indignant and bitter.

What REALLY Causes Negative Thinking and What Can You Do About It?

Do you find which you get caught up for your head — thinking, churning, and ruminating? If the solution is yes and you were to continue along the usually typical direction for coping with your poor wondering, you'll locate yourself difficult and struggling with your wondering, getting stuck in to exchange your negative thoughts to superb thoughts. Due to the fact, it entails greater wondering, and that typically leaves us feeling worse and requires a tremendous quantity of power and practice. So what's the answer?

First, allows apprehend what reasons bad wondering to strengthen, then we will start to paintings at the purpose. There are three predominant triggers of elevated wondering activity: the primary we can work with, the 1/3 we simply need to recognize.

Earlier than I communicate about those three causes, let me be clear and say that I'm speaking approximately conscious mind – mind you can hit upon, the chattering inner talk which you are privy to whilst you area your interest on it. This aware thought isn't the same as subconscious 'ideals' or 'value determinations,' which exist at a distinct degree. Aware mind is a slower denser vibration as compared to subconscious 'ideals', which are a better lighter vibration.

Observe our causes:

Dependency: the more we suppose, the more we assume. In spite of that sounding ludicrously obvious, it is an easy fact that we are creatures of addiction, and the extra time we spend with our interest and energy in our questioning brain, the more we will gravitate closer to spending time in our heads thinking.

There's little doubt that as a way of life, a great deal of our attention and electricity is in our head. We have a tendency to be engaged in one hobby at the same time as considering the following few things we will be doing. Studying, comparing, and generally overthinking is not unusual. But, this is an addiction that may be broken via redirecting interest. Being greater present inside the now second and reconnecting with the bodily frame are very beneficial ways of breaking this addiction.

The Presence of Emotion: emotion is a complex physiological process that influences the entire frame and all of the brain. Whilst emotion is present inside the frame and brain, the thinking facilities of the mind come to be more active. So in case you be aware your questioning ramping up, in particular, if it's far bad questioning, there is a great chance that there may be emotion inside you looking to get your attention. Doing something with the emotion and taking some movement is considerably higher than trying to manage your questioning.

You in no way want to reflect on consideration of emotion. As such, you absolutely need just to accept it, sense it, and act on it wherein appropriate. The maximum of the thinking that follows emotion is an try to break out the emotion, to resist it, and get away from it as rapid as viable thru evaluation and explanation. Mastering to, without a doubt, take a seat with emotion without having to break out; it could be effective and profound.

Thought power: that is where we get a touch esoteric. Carl Jung mentioned the collective subconscious, and Rupert Sheldrake talks about morphic fields, so I'm going to attract these thoughts. Permit's think about our brains as antennae that track into quantum fields – almost just like the manner our television sets acquire and transmit rather than generate the sign. Try and believe that strength exists inside quantum mass awareness fields, and our brains pick out upon this power and then convert it to thoughts. These thoughts aren't our own; they seem to land in our brains. This isn't something we can necessarily manage, and there seems to be something of a drift of them inside and out of our brains. But, if we're choosing up on lots of undesirable 'mass cognizance' mind, it's far something of a mirrored image of our personal vibrational kingdom. So, while you feel related to yourself and you are in a 'space' of love, compassion, and gratitude, you'll find that there may be appreciably much less wondering hobby taking area and less mind touchdown to your brain. Conversely, whilst you are a nation of fear or anger – lower vibrational states – your receiver-brain will pick up on extra undesirable concept-electricity because it floats through your focus.

What we are able to do is recognize the presence of this mass recognition mind and permit them to drift through without giving them too much time or interest.

The first step in gaining mastery of your thinking is to apprehend in which a lot of your conscious concept comes from. Remember that difficult thinking and battling it head-on aren't the answers. Being present within the now in your frame and acting in alignment together with your deeper feelings will bring about a sizeable discount in what can seem like steady intellectual chatter.

Chapter 5

Treatment for Panic Attacks

In many managed studies experiments through the years, human beings with panic were given (a) social capabilities and educative training, (b) psychotherapy, (c) relaxation, meditative, and mindfulness schooling, (d) hypnosis, (e) medicine best, and (f) cognitive-behavioral therapy. In each of those studies, there has been a management organization.

In particular, whilst the intention became to help humans "triumph over" panic and panic attacks, cognitive-behavioral remedy was the handiest therapy to show enormous results. Cognitive-behavioral remedy additionally showed effectiveness (efficacy) whilst blended with rest, meditation, and mindfulness schooling. Even though relaxation and meditative training, while mixed with cognitive-behavioral remedy has been proven to paintings, it does now not paintings without the predominant element -- cognitive-behavioral remedy. This is relaxation, meditation, and mindfulness are secondary adjuncts to CBT.

Cognitive treatment for panic sickness consists of getting the person to peer themselves and the sector around them realistically. Rational wondering is cautiously taught, and emotional reasoning is tested and reduced. The paradoxical nature of panic and tension are brought, and the patient is consistently bombarded with rational thoughts and commonplace feel reasoning. Techniques to calm down are taught and made sensible, in order that the patient knows a way to relax in actual life conditions.

The cognitive and behavioral therapy works when the affected person is inspired to get higher and inclined to work on changing their lifestyles. CBT does no longer work for folks who are not stimulated and will no longer do the therapy. This has been every other locating from studies experiments and clinical revel in people that honestly do the remedy get higher, while those who are not prompted to do the therapy do now not get higher. Although that is as you'll count on, it pulls the success fee down substantially. Controlling for motivation earlier than the beginning of a observe might substantially enhance posted achievement prices for cognitive-behavioral therapy.

Behavioral remedy emphasizes honestly calming down in traumatic situations. As an example, a panic remedy institution practices those strategies with the aid of keeping a mock conference where they have to speak with different humans they've never met. The goal is to use the calming down techniques they have discovered to live comfy and calm, instead of letting tension and panic take manage. Behavioral therapy is likewise being hired when the stirrings of a panic assault are felt, and those reply in specific methods than they've in the beyond. Behavioral remedy for panic includes setting into place what has been learned in cognitive remedy.

One without the alternative does no longer work. Cognitive therapy adjustments the manner someone thinks completely, and behavioral remedy modifications the way someone acts. Each are critical elements to the answer of panic and tension.

Remedy for Panic disorders

Treating tension issues with remedy

Whether or not you're stricken by panic attacks, obsessive mind, unrelenting concerns, or an incapacitating phobia, it's critical to understand that you ought not to stay with anxiety and worry. Treatment can help, and for many tension troubles, remedy is frequently the simplest choice. That's due to the fact anxiety remedy—not like tension medicine—treats more than simply the signs of the trouble. Remedy allows you to uncover the underlying causes of your worries and fears; discover ways to relax; observe situations in new, much less frightening approaches; and increase better coping and problem-fixing abilities. Remedy gives you the equipment to overcome anxiety and teaches you the way to use them.

Tension problems range appreciably, so therapy has to be tailored in your unique signs and symptoms and diagnosis. When you have obsessive-compulsive sickness (OCD), as an example, your remedy might be unique from someone who wishes help for anxiety assaults. The duration of therapy may also rely on the sort and severity of your tension disorder. But, many tension treatment options are an exceptionally quick-time period. In keeping with the Yankee psychological affiliation, many people enhance considerably within eight to ten therapy classes.

While many different varieties of remedies are used to deal with tension, the leading strategies are cognitive behavioral therapy (CBT) and publicity therapy. Each anxiety therapy may be used by yourself or combined with different kinds of therapy. Tension therapy may be performed in my view, or it may take region in a group of people with comparable tension troubles.

But the purpose is equal: to decrease your anxiety degrees, calm your mind, and conquer your fears.

Cognitive-behavioral therapy (CBT) for anxiety

Cognitive-behavioral remedy (CBT) is the maximum widely-used therapy for tension problems. Studies have shown it to be effective inside the treatment of the panic ailment, phobias, social anxiety disorder, and generalized tension sickness, among many other situations.

CBT addresses bad patterns and distortions inside the way we look at the world and ourselves. As the call indicates, this involves two primary components:

Cognitive therapy examines how terrible thoughts, or cognitions, make contributions to anxiety.

Conduct remedy examines the way you behave and react in conditions that cause anxiety.

The basic premise of CBT is that our thoughts—no longer outside occasions—has an effect on the way we experience. In other phrases, it's no longer the situation you're in that determines the way you feel; however, your belief of the state of affairs. As an instance, believe which you've simply been invited to a huge celebration. Remember three unique methods of considering the invitation and the way that mind might have an effect on your emotions.

As you could see, the identical event can cause completely extraordinary emotions in distinctive human beings. It all relies upon on our individual expectations, attitudes, and beliefs for humans with anxiety problems, bad approach of thinking gasoline the poor feelings of anxiety and worry. The aim of the cognitive-behavioral remedy for anxiety is to discover and correct those negative minds and ideals. The concept is that in case you trade the manner you believe you studied, you may trade the way you sense.

Notion tough in CBT for anxiety

Notion hard—also known as cognitive restructuring—is a manner in that you task the negative thinking styles that make a contribution to your tension, changing them with extra effective, realistic thoughts. This involves three steps:

With anxiety issues, situations are perceived as extra risky as they really are. To a person with a germ phobia, as an instance, shaking every other man or woman's hand can seem life-threatening. Although you may effortlessly see that this is an irrational fear, figuring out your own irrational, scary thoughts may be very hard. One method is to invite yourself to what you have been thinking whilst you began feeling irritating. Your therapist will assist you with this step.

In the 2nd step, your therapist will educate you on the way to compare your anxiety-upsetting mind. This involves questioning the evidence in your frightening thoughts, analyzing unhelpful ideas, and trying out out the reality of poor predictions. Strategies for tough, poor minds include conducting experiments, weighing the pros and cons of stressful or averting the aspect you worry, and determining the sensible possibilities that what you're annoying approximately will surely occur.

The irrational predictions and terrible distortions on your annoying thoughts, you could update them with the new mind, which is more correct and superb. Your therapist may also help you give you realistic, calming statements you could say to yourself whilst you're facing or looking ahead to a state of affairs that normally sends your tension degrees hovering.

To understand how difficult idea works in cognitive behavioral remedy, remember the subsequent example: Maria gained take the subway due to the fact she's afraid she'll skip out, after which everyone will suppose she's crazy. Her therapist has asked her to put in writing down her negative thoughts, pick out the errors—or cognitive distortions—in her questioning, and come up with a greater rational interpretation. The effects are under.

Changing a negative mind with greater realistic ones is simpler stated than performed. Often, negative thoughts are part of a lifelong sample of questioning. It takes exercise to break the habit. That's why cognitive-behavioral remedy includes working towards your very own at domestic as nicely. CBT may additionally include:

Studying to apprehend when you're annoying and what that feels like in the frame

Gaining knowledge of coping competencies and relaxation techniques to counteract tension and panic

Confronting your fears (both for your imagination or in actual life)

Exposure therapy for anxiety

Tension isn't a pleasing sensation, so it's best natural to avoid it if you could. One of the approaches that people do this is by using steering clean of the conditions that make them stressful. When you have a fear of heights, you might power 3 hours from your way to keep away from crossing a tall bridge. Or if the prospect of public speaking leaves your belly in knots, you may skip your first-rate buddy's wedding ceremony, which will avoid giving a toast. Other than the inconvenience aspect, the trouble with averting your fears is that you by no means have the hazard to overcome them. In fact, avoiding your fears frequently makes them more potent.

Exposure therapy, as the call suggests, exposes you to the situations or gadgets you worry about. The idea is that through repeated exposures, you'll feel an increasing feel of manipulate over the situation, and your anxiety will diminish. The publicity is done in certainly one of two approaches: Your therapist may ask you to assume the frightening situation, or you can confront it in actual existence. Publicity therapy may be used on my own, or it is able to be performed as part of the cognitive-behavioral remedy.

Systematic desensitization

Rather than going through your biggest fear right away, which can be traumatizing, publicity therapy typically starts with a state of affairs that's best mildly threatening and works up from there. This step-through-step method is called systematic desensitization. Systematic desensitization allows you to progressively task your fears, construct self-assurance, and master talents for controlling panic.

First, your therapist will teach you a relaxation approach, consisting of modern muscle relaxation or deep respiratory. You'll exercise in a remedy and for your personal at home. Once you begin confronting your fears, you'll use this rest technique to lessen your physical anxiety reaction (consisting of trembling and hyperventilating) and inspire relaxation.

Next, you'll create a listing of 10 to 20 scary situations that progress closer to your very last intention. As an instance, if your final goal is to triumph over your fear of flying, you would possibly start through looking at pictures of planes and end with taking an actual flight. Every step needs to be as particular as possible, with a clear, measurable goal.

Underneath the guidance of your therapist, you'll then begin to work via the list. The goal is to live in each horrifying scenario until your fears subside. That manner, you'll examine that the feelings gained hurt you and that they do go away. On every occasion, the tension receives too extreme, and you will switch to the relaxation technique you learned. Once you're comfy once more, you may turn your interest returned to the scenario. In this way, you'll find paintings through the steps until you're capable of finishing each one without feeling overly distressed.

Complementary treatment plans for tension problems

As you discover your anxiety ailment in remedy, you may also want to test with complementary treatment options designed to convey your standard stress degrees down and assist you obtain emotional stability.

Exercising is a natural stress buster and anxiety reliever. Studies indicate that as little as half-hour of exercise three to 5 instances per week can provide vast anxiety comfort. To obtain the maximum advantage, purpose for at least an hour of aerobic exercise on most days.

Rest strategies, which include mindfulness meditation and modern muscle relaxation, while practiced frequently, can lessen tension and growth feelings of emotional nicely-being.

Biofeedback uses sensors that measure precise physiological functions—which includes coronary heart rate, respiration, and muscle anxiety—to teach you to apprehend your frame's tension response and discover ways to manipulate it the usage of relaxation strategies.

Hypnosis is occasionally used in aggregate with CBT for tension. While you're in a country of deep rest, the hypnotherapist makes use of exceptional healing techniques to help you face your fears and observe them in new ways.

There's no short restore for anxiety. Overcoming a tension disease takes time and dedication. Therapy includes facing your fears as opposed to keeping off them, so once in a while, you'll feel worse before you get better. The vital issue is to stick with remedy and follow your therapist's recommendation. In case you're feeling discouraged with the pace of restoration, understand that therapy for anxiety may be very effective in the long run. You'll obtain the advantages if you see it thru.

You can additionally support your personal tension therapy through making high quality picks. The entirety out of your interest level to your social life affects tension. Set the degree for fulfillment by means of making a conscious choice to promote rest, energy, and an effective intellectual outlook to your ordinary existence.

Domesticate your connections with different people. Loneliness and isolation set the level of tension. Lower your vulnerability by means of attaining out to others. Make it a point to peer pals; be part of a self-help or aid organization; share your issues and issues with a trusted cherished one.

Adopt healthy lifestyle behavior. Physical activity relieves tension and anxiety, so find time for ordinary exercise. Don't use alcohol and pills to address your symptoms and try to keep away from stimulants consisting of caffeine and nicotine, which can make anxiety worse.

A way to deal with stress evidently

Many humans have persistent pressure and anxiety. They face signs and symptoms such as anxiousness, agitation, anxiety, a racing heart, and chest ache.

In truth, anxiety is among the maximum common mental health troubles. Within America, more than 18 percentage of adults are affected by tension disorders every yr.

In a few instances, every other fitness condition, which includes an overactive thyroid, can result in a tension disorder. Getting a correct diagnosis can ensure that a person gets a quality remedy.

Herbal remedies for tension and stress

Natural treatments are generally secure to use alongside greater conventional scientific healing procedures.

But, alterations to the weight-reduction plan and a few natural dietary supplements can exchange the manner antianxiety medications paintings, so it is critical to consult a health practitioner before attempting these solutions. The physician will also be capable of advise other herbal treatments.

1. Exercise

Exercise is a tremendous manner of burning off disturbing power, and studies have a tendency to assist this use.

For instance, a 2015 evaluation of 12 randomized managed trials found that exercise can be a treatment for tension. However, the evaluation advised that the simplest studies of better exceptional could determine how effective it's far.

Exercise may additionally help with tension resulting from disturbing circumstances. Results of a 2016 take a look at, for instance, suggest that exercise can advantage humans with tension associated with quitting smoking.

2. Meditation

Meditation can assist in a sluggish racing mind, making it less difficult to manage pressure and tension. A wide variety of meditation styles, consisting of mindfulness and meditation in the course of yoga, can also help.

Mindfulness-primarily based meditation is increasingly more popular in therapy. A 2010 meta-analytic assessment shows that it may be relatively powerful for human beings with disorders regarding temper and anxiety.

3. Relaxation sports

mendacity in a relaxed role and slowly constricting and relaxing every muscle group, starting with theft and operating as much as the shoulders and jaw.

4. Writing

Finding a way to specific tension can make it feel more doable.

Some research indicates that journaling and other kinds of writing can assist humans in coping higher with tension.

2016 take a look at, as an example, located that creative writing can also assist children and teens in manipulating tension.

5. Time management strategies

These may contain their own family, paintings, and fitness-associated sports. Having a plan in location for the subsequent essential motion can help to hold this tension at bay.

Effective time control techniques can assist human beings in focusing on one assignment at a time. Ebook-primarily based planners and online calendars can assist, as can resisting the urge to multitask.

Some humans discover that breaking main projects down into practicable steps can assist them in performing the obligations of the one with less pressure.

6. Aromatherapy

Smelling soothing plant oils can assist in easing pressure and anxiety. Sure, scents paintings higher for some people than others, so consider experimenting with numerous alternatives.

Lavender may be, in particular helpful. A 2012 study examined the outcomes of aromatherapy with lavender on insomnia in sixty-seven women aged 45–fifty-five. Results endorse that aromatherapy may also lessen the coronary heart fee inside the quick-term and assist in easing sleep problems in a long time.

7. Cannabidiol oil

CBD oil comes from the marijuana plant.

Cannabidiol (CBD) oil is a by-product of the hashish or marijuana plant.

CBD oil is without problems to be had without a prescription in many opportunity healthcare shops. Initial research indicates that it has widespread capacity to reduce anxiety and panic.

In areas where clinical marijuana is a felony, docs can also be capable of prescribing the oil.

8. Natural teas

Many herbal teas promise to help with tension and simplicity sleep.

A few human beings discover the technique of creating and drinking tea soothing, but a few teas may also have an extra direct effect at the mind that consequences in decreased tension.

Consequences of a small 2018 trial recommend that chamomile can adjust ranges of cortisol, a pressure hormone.

9. Herbal supplements

Like natural teas, many natural supplements declare to reduce tension. However, little clinical proof supports those claims.

It's far vital to paintings with a health practitioner who is informed approximately herbal supplements and their ability interactions with other drugs.

10. Time with animals

Pets provide companionship, love, and assistance. Research published in 2018 showed that pets might be beneficial to humans with a variety of intellectual health troubles, inclusive of tension.

At the same time, as many people select cats, dogs, and other small mammals, people with allergic reactions can be thrilled to study that the pet does need to be bushy to offer support.

When in doubt, shout It Out! Eight Drug-loose approaches to conflict anxiety

Among paintings, bills, circle of relatives, and seeking to stay wholesome, the everyday pressures of life can flip you into a traumatic mess. Maybe you have been an aggravating baby who grew into a traumatic person, or perhaps you evolved tension later in existence. Regardless of while symptoms started, it's feasible that your mind is in overdrive, and also you're continually anticipating the rug to be pulled out from beneath you.

You're no longer alone. In line with the tension and despair association of the United States, tension problems are the maximum common intellectual infection inside America, affecting forty million adults. Like so many others seeking out comfort, you may have become to remedy for help. Despite the fact that antianxiety tablets can ease your anxiety, the serenity can come with a fee tag inside the shape of facet outcomes. Trouble sleeping, reduced libido, jumpiness, and expanded starvation are a number of the most not unusual inconveniences of treating anxiety with drugs.

The good information is that popping drugs isn't the only manner to get your fears and nerves under manipulate. Right here are eight easy and powerful approaches to warfare tension without medication.

1. Shout it out

This doesn't mean setting fear in others so that they experience on facet such as you. We are talking approximately a healthy release of emotions in a managed environment. The extra you combat anxiety, the more overwhelming it may emerge as. Instead, include tension as a part of your lifestyles, after which permit it to go. Scream at the pinnacle of your lungs, punch a pillow, stomp your ft, or pound your chest. Does something allow you to get it out! One I. A.-based yoga trainer even evolved a category referred to as Tantrum Yoga that encourages yogis to strive these unconventional techniques as a way to release emotion that "receives caught in our bodies and could turn into strain, ailment, and many others."

2. Get shifting

Exercising might be the closing aspect you need to do whilst your mind's in overdrive. You could fear publish-workout pain and being unable to walk or sit for the next two days. Or your account may go to the worst-case scenario, and you worry overexerting yourself and having a coronary heart attack. But in reality, exercising is one of the great herbal antianxiety solutions.

Physical hobby raises endorphins and serotonin degrees that will help you experience higher emotions. And when you experience better at the inside, your whole outlook improves. And because your brain can't make recognition similarly on two matters at once, exercise can also take your thoughts off your problems. Don't suppose you have to battle via a painful task. Any kind of motion is right, so put on your preferred jam and circulate across the residence. Or grab a mat and break out into your favorite yoga poses.

3. Breakdown up with caffeine

A cup of espresso, chocolate, or an ice-cold Coke might help you experience better. But if caffeine is your move-to drug of desire, your tension could worsen.

Caffeine gives the apprehensive gadget a jolt that can improve electricity ranges. But while under pressure, this anxious strength can induce an anxiety assault. Now, the concept of giving up your preferred caffeinated beverage would possibly enhance your coronary heart rate and produce tension as you examine this, but you don't must prevent bloodless turkey or give up caffeine completely. It's all approximately moderation.

4. Supply yourself a bedtime

Along with your busy time table, there's no time for sleep, proper? Some workaholics brag approximately most effective needing three or 4 hours of sleep a night, as though to say, "I'm greater determined and dedicated than everybody else." but irrespective of what you would possibly tell yourself, you're not a robotic. People need sleep to characteristic properly, so unless you beamed in from some close by planet, this also applies to you.

Whether you cope with insomnia, purposely limit your quantity of sleep; otherwise, you're a self-professed night time owl; chronic sleep deprivation makes you vulnerable to anxiety. Do yourself (and absolutely everyone around you) a prefer and get 8 to nine hours of sleep every night. Develop a bedtime recurring to read an e-book or do something enjoyable earlier than mattress. The better organized you are to get an excellent night's sleep, the higher the fine of sleep you'll have, which results in a better morning as nicely.

5. Feel adequate saying no

Your plate is best so big, and if you weigh down yourself with each person else's personal issues, your anxiety may also get worse. We've all heard the adage, "There's greater happiness in giving than receiving." however, nowhere on this sentence does it say you should take a seat back and allow others to infringe on your time.

Whether you're driving a person round on errands, choosing up their youngsters from school, or lending an ear approximately their troubles, you'll have little electricity to care for your personal affairs if you spend almost all of your power being concerned for others. This doesn't mean you must in no way assist everyone; however, understand your boundaries, and don't be afraid to mention "no" whilst you want to.

6. Don't bypass food

If anxiety causes nausea, the notion of ingesting food is as attractive as eating dirt. However, skipping a meal could make anxiety worse. Your blood sugar drops while you don't eat, which reasons the release of a pressure hormone referred to as cortisol. Cortisol will let you perform better beneath pressure; however, it may additionally make your experience worse in case you're already liable to tension.

The truth that you need to consume does not justify stuffing simply whatever for your mouth, so this isn't always an excuse to overindulge in sugar and junk food. Sugar doesn't motive tension; however, a sugar rush can reason bodily signs and symptoms of hysteria, consisting of anxiety and shaking. And in case you start to obsess over a reaction to sugar, you may have an out-all panic attack.

Incorporate more lean proteins, fruits, greens, and healthful fat into your eating regimen. Devour five to six small foods all through the day, and avoid or limit your consumption of sugar and refined carbohydrates.

How to Fight Anxiety without Medication

What is Anxiety?

Absolutely everyone receives nerve-racking every so often, whether there is a hard take a look at faculty, monetary troubles, family drama, or a piece cut-off date. That is every day, but it can nevertheless prevent us from getting a fantastic night time sleep.

An anxiety ailment, on the other hand, is while tension begins to continually intrude along with your capacity to lead a healthy life. Anxiety problems can reason constant and overwhelming fear and fear. There are numerous styles of anxiety disorders, along with however not restrained to:

Generalized anxiety disorder (GAD)

Panic sickness is recognized in those who experience spontaneous, apparently, out-of-the-blue panic assaults and is preoccupied with the worry of a fixed charge. Panic assaults arise all at once, every so often even all through sleep.

Phobia

A constant and unreasonable fear as a result of the presence or idea of a specific object or state of affairs that generally poses little or no danger. Publicity to the object or scenario brings about an immediate reaction, causing the individual to endure excessive anxiety or to keep away from the purpose or state of affairs altogether.

Put up-traumatic stress ailment (PTSD)

Publish demanding pressure disease is a critical doubtlessly debilitating condition that can arise in humans who have experienced or witnessed a herbal catastrophe, final twist of fate, terrorist incident, unexpected loss of life of a cherished one, struggle, violent personal assault, or other lifestyles-threatening occasion. Symptoms can consist of tension, depression, flashbacks, and nightmares.

Those conditions frequently require help and treatment from scientific specialists and can be the purpose of frequent episodes of terrible sleep.

Deal with anxiety clearly without medicine

There are quite some clean, herbal ways to lessen tension and help you go to sleep quicker. But before we get there, it's precise to understand why we need to don't forget treating anxiety without prescription medication.

First, anti-tension medications may have some severe facet outcomes. For instance, selective serotonin reuptake inhibitors (SSRIs) like Zoloft, Prozac, and Paxil are used to deal with despair and anxiety with the aid of increasing tiers of serotonin within the mind; these can have some severe aspect effects including nausea, insomnia, diarrhea, nervousness, emotional numbness, blunted emotions and sexual dysfunction to call some.

Second, the latest research shows that, for anxiety problems, short time period structured learning-based remedies (like Cognitive Behavioral therapy) often outperform remedy remedies. This is, in particular, proper for long-time period consequences. By teaching your brain now not to panic, you deal with the purpose as opposed to the symptoms. Analyze more fabulous about Cognitive Behavioral therapy here.

Even if you do now not have an anxiety sickness, schooling yourself to conquer terrible, annoying thoughts will assist make absolute peace of thoughts and restful sleep for an entire life.

Treat anxiety with respiratory: It's that easy

While you are feeling burdened and aggravating, you may word a few familiar, however uncomfortable signs and symptoms: your muscle groups demanding, your respiratory becomes shallow and fast, and your heart beats more excellent speedy.. That is your body preparing to reply to a danger, actual or imagined, via the "fight or flight" response. This response is as an alternative beneficial if you have to combat off or flee from a endure inside the woods.

Practical, deep breathing exercises are an easy way to inform your body that there is no actual danger. Bottomless, gradual stomach respiratory using your diaphragm activates the parasympathetic anxious system (chargeable for "rest and digest" mode), which relaxes us. Even as yogis have long due to the fact included breathwork, or pranayama, into their practice to intentionally manipulate temper and electricity ranges, you don't need to be a respiratory expert to inform your body to relax. Yogis name it dirge pranayama; it entails locating a relaxed function, then breathing in deeply and slowly, first into the stomach, then the ribcage, then into the pinnacle of the chest. Exhale in the opposite order: first out of the crest of the chest, then the ribcage, then the lowest of the stomach. And repeat! Integrative fitness professional Dr. Weil teaches a comparable respiratory method, the 4–7–8 Breath, which locations much less emphasis at the place of the breath and more attention on the timing of the breath (four seconds of inhaling, 7 seconds of breath-protecting, and 8 seconds of exhaling). Attempt both to peer who works excellent for you!

Reduce anxiety with exercising

This isn't information, possibly; however, exercise is a notable strain-reliever! In keeping with the tension and melancholy affiliation of the united states, researchers have observed that "regular participation in aerobic exercising has been proven to lower normal degrees of tension, raise and stabilize mood, enhance sleep, and enhance self-esteem." do not forget the stress hormone adrenaline launched from your "combat-or-flight" response? Exercising naturally reduces this hormone, permitting your body to return right into a nation of equilibrium and relaxation. Further, bodily pastime facilitates release those feel-suitable neurotransmitters known as endorphins, making you feel happier and much less annoying. Aerobic activities also have the brought gain of permitting you to think about something aside from what you might be involved about, serving as a form of active meditation.

You don't want to run a marathon to get the blessings of exercise, either. Cross on a hike, go to a yoga consultation, or play a sport of tennis with a friend — something you revel in! Any shape of workout will assist with stress management, and also you'll get all of the different introduced health benefits at the side of it.

Meditation and Mindfulness to control tension

Happily, we don't have to practice meditation for 34,000 hours to prevent stress. At Wake wooded area college of medicine, Fadel Zeidan and Robert C. Coghill located that after just four days of 20-minute exercise of mindfulness meditation (the Buddhist practice known as shamatha), volunteers reported a 57% reduction in ache unpleasantness to a warm probe stimulus. After the handiest four days, volunteers' brains had started to reply to the meditative practice! Like several enterprises, the higher you exercise, the less complicated it turns into, and the better you will be.

But, in which to begin? It's far essential to locate the nice one which fits your needs and spirituality. Dr. Elizabeth Hoge, psychiatrist at the center for tension and difficult pressure issues at Massachusetts, well-known sanatorium, recommends mindfulness meditation for treating anxiety. For novices, study the meditation fundamentals and search the numerous websites, YouTube motion pictures, and apps that offer meditation education. For those laid low with extra severe anxiety or chronic pain, keep in mind a path in Mindfulness-based totally stress discounts through your healthcare provider. It's far perhaps no surprise that MBSR has been discovered to be very active within the treatment of anxiety disorders.

Herbal Anti-anxiety foods and dietary supplements

With all the ingredients, teas, nutritional supplements, and nutraceuticals to be had to "treat" tension, it's tough to decide what works and what purely snake oil is. Our studies indicate there are some consumables which can help with anxiety; here is what we found:

Meals

Having a generally healthy weight loss plan with all the proper ingredients and nutrients is a superb place to begin to save you tension. We all understand the sensation of being "hangry": traumatic, jittery, and irritable due to the fact we haven't eaten these days. Be sure to devour enough proteins and complicated carbohydrates to maintain blood sugar regularly during the day.

Some research proposes eating meals rich in omega-three fatty acids can lessen tension. It's undoubtedly really worth an attempt because those meals are delicious and assist keep off heart ailment! The ingredients maximum in omega-three fatty acids consists of flaxseeds, fish like salmon and mackerel, walnuts, edamame and tofu, chia seeds, and oysters.

The amino acid tryptophan is the concept to play a crucial function in our brain chemistry, which includes tension and melancholy due to the fact it's far a precursor to the neurotransmitters serotonin and melatonin. Tryptophan dietary supplements are marketed to assist with tension; however, their efficacy is unproven. Such a lot of foods are already high in tryptophan (like eggs, spiraling kinds of pasta, codfish, soybeans, hen, and oats), that with a healthful, numerous eating regimens, it's far probable that you are already getting enough tryptophan.

Supplements

In the latest years, researchers have started exploring the connection between wholesome intestine flora (the right balance of "suitable" microorganism in your digestive tract) and intellectual health. Yes, you read that efficiently. Healthful gut bacteria may be a way to save you anxiety. In a study at Oxford University, neuroscientists observed that when taking "prebiotics" (non-digestible fiber compounds that are food for precise microorganism) for three weeks, topics were capable of greater without difficulty forget about poor stimuli and pay extra interest to positive stimuli. In other words, after taking prebiotic supplements, topics have been much less demanding while given terrible records. Subjects additionally had lower degrees of cortisol, a strain hormone-related to tension, in their systems. Likewise, another French has a look at established that, after two weeks, the management of dietary supplements with probiotic stress s reduced anxiety-like behavior in take a look at rats and also alleviated mental distress in human volunteers. Probiotics and prebiotics may be eaten as food or taken as dietary supplements. Meals excessive in probiotics include sauerkraut, sourdough bread, kefir and yogurt, miso soup, tempeh, and tender cheeses. Ingredients high in prebiotics are chicory root, dandelion veggies, Jerusalem artichoke, garlic, onions, asparagus, bananas, leeks, oats, and barley.

Natural remedies

Some herbal herbs and spices have proven promise inside the remedy of hysteria as properly. While many homeopathic herbs are bought on-line and in stores, not they all were scientifically studied or observed to be powerful for treating anxiety. Many web sites recommend skullcap, ashwagandha, valerian, St. John's Wart, and ginkgo Biloba; however, most studies have now not shown their efficacy. Chamomile tea can also assist reduce anxiety a modest amount. Passionflower has additionally been shown to have a positive effect on the signs and symptoms of hysteria issues. Kava root extract has been confirmed to reduce tension greatly; but, other studies have indicated that it can reason liver damage, so its use isn't always typically advocated by way of scientific specialists. Make certain to speak about any herbal supplements along with your health practitioner to avoid destructive reactions with different medications.

In case you appear to stay in one of the U.S. States that has legalized medicinal marijuana, then possibly you have taken into consideration the use of scientific marijuana for tension? In spite of everything, tetrahydro cannabinoid (THC), one of the chemical compounds in marijuana, is well known to create the brief satisfied, at ease, feeling we would associate with the drug. However, to date, research had been limited as to the outcomes of marijuana on tension disorders of the few research; some have indicated that marijuana might also make tension signs of panic and paranoia worse, and long term use may additionally sooner or later reason memory loss and cognitive impairment. For quick time use, reactions to the drug range, some discover marijuana with low doses of THC very relaxing. Again, make sure to speak with your doctor approximately using marijuana to deal with tension efficiently.